AF841171

FROM VICTIM TO VICTOR

FROM VICTIM TO VICTOR

Conquering Financial Fraud, Overcoming Shame and Emerging Stronger

Amelia Parker

Cherish
EDITIONS

First published in Great Britain 2024 by Cherish Editions
Cherish Editions is a trading style of Shaw Callaghan Ltd &
Shaw Callaghan 23 USA, INC.

The Stanley Building, 7 Pancras Square
King's Cross
London
N1C 4AG
www.triggerhub.org

Text Copyright © 2024 Amelia Parker

All rights reserved. No part of this publication may be reproduced, stored in a retrieval system, or transmitted in any form or by any means, electronic, mechanical, photocopying, recording or otherwise, without prior permission in writing from the publisher

British Library Cataloguing in Publication Data
A CIP catalogue record for this book is available upon
request from the British Library
ISBN: 978-1-916920-74-3

This book is also available in the following eBook formats:
ePUB: 978-1-916920-75-0

Amelia Parker has asserted her right under the Copyright, Design and Patents Act 1988 to be identified as the author of this work

Cover design by More Visual
Typeset by Lapiz Digital Services

CONTENTS

INTRODUCTION

Offers that seem too good to be true are often part of a larger deception plan.

– Ron Weber

In June 2020, I stumbled upon what seemed like an incredible investment opportunity. The reviews were overwhelmingly positive, and the person behind them exuded charm and charisma. Intrigued, I dipped my toes into the investment pool by initially investing a small amount to verify its legitimacy. I was completely unprepared for the journey that lay ahead.

Discovering the investment initially filled me with immense excitement. It felt like a remarkable stroke of luck, providing a welcome distraction from the recent loss of my mother and my husband's diagnosis. Though it seemed almost too good to be true, I required little persuasion to invest, as it ignited a spark of hope for my and my family's future.

It was a rollercoaster of emotions that accompanied these heart-wrenching personal developments. From the suffocating weight of grief to the shocking diagnosis that felt like a gut punch, I was raw and caught in the crosshairs of life's most devastating blows. This book follows my journey of vulnerability and strength as I navigated the stormy seas of my emotions, searching for a glimmer of hope amidst the darkness and uncertainty. I will recount the harrowing moments when I discovered the depths of my resilience in the face of unimaginable challenges.

It's amazing how quickly someone who is esteemed for their knowledge, dependability, toughness and sensibility can find themselves in total disarray. I was known among my colleagues as the go-to expert in my field, and my friends considered me the poster child for wisdom and reliability. The moment I grasped that I had fallen victim to a scam, my entire world crumbled as if I were trapped in an inescapable nightmare.

It's a bit like watching a superhero lose their powers overnight, except in my case, I wasn't battling supervillains, but scam artists in disguise. But when the fraud hit, it was as if my "super-sensible" cape had been yanked away, leaving me feeling more like a befuddled sidekick than a leading lady.

I felt helpless and overwhelmed when I realized that fraudsters had tricked and manipulated me. It was as though the very foundation of trust and security I had built over many years had crumbled beneath me. This unexpected turn of events felt like a relentless horror show with no exit in sight.

Amid this turmoil, I found solace in the support of my closest friends and family. They offered a lifeline of empathy and understanding when I felt most vulnerable. They were my emotional safety net, my human version of a fluffy pillow. It was a stark reminder that even the most resilient and dependable individuals can be susceptible to the cunning tactics of scammers.

As I began to piece everything together in the aftermath of the scam, I realized that this experience, though overwhelming and deeply painful, had the potential to teach me valuable lessons about vigilance, trust and resilience. It was a journey toward regaining not only my financial security, but also my emotional wellbeing, and it underscored the importance of staying informed and cautious in an increasingly complex digital world. Ultimately, this rollercoaster journey turned out to be a valuable experience, like a crash course in life's irrationality.

Currently, my fraud case is under active investigation by the police, and it is scheduled to proceed to court in 2024. To maintain the integrity of the ongoing legal process, I have refrained from disclosing the names of the fraudsters and key company details. My case is part of a much larger, long-standing fraud case spanning several years. This impending trial is anticipated to be significant and far-reaching, and I will play a pivotal role as a key witness.

I sincerely hope that justice will be served, leading to the conviction of the fraudsters responsible for not only upending my life, but also impacting numerous others' lives, too.

Why This Book Is Necessary

We all know that fraud happens – we just don't know to what extent. The truth is that it is much more common than we realize. We only ever hear about the major incidents that generate headlines, such as the Anna Sorokin scandal, in which the fraudster masqueraded as a wealthy German heiress and defrauded the socialites of New York of their money. Or the tale of Elizabeth Holmes, the creator and ex-CEO of the health technology startup Theranos, who claimed to have transformed blood testing with her device, which required only a few drops to run a number of life-saving tests. But as time went on, it became clear that the business had been a fraud – only after Holmes and other senior team members stole millions of dollars from investors.

While these stories are fascinating and important to tell, so are the millions of other cases where ordinary people get scammed out of their hard-earned money. These stories are just as valuable to us, and not just for the sake of having others feel sorry for us or gaining some notoriety. It's because we know that power comes from knowledge. A big part of the reason why scammers feel so confident in their acts is because for the most part, they get away with it.

To me, the phrase "con artist" basically means "confidence game". Scammers are so incredibly confident, not just during the scam, but also after it, once they've already gotten the money, because most people never report it. This is usually due to a number of different factors, like feeling stupid and embarrassed for falling for the scam, not knowing what steps to take once you've been defrauded, and not knowing how to deal with the mixed emotions of being scammed.

Luckily, this book covers all of that! Not only will I recount my personal experience as a fraud victim who ultimately emerged victorious, but I will also impart knowledge regarding the process by which con artists select and prepare their targets. We'll also examine the typical strategies con artists employ to trick and bait their victims. Not ending there, I'll also touch on the common types of scams to watch out for and how to detect them. This book also offers advice on what to do if you've recently learned that you've been scammed or are about to be scammed so that you may be able to get your money back.

We'll also talk about the telltale signs that someone is a scammer, and the early warning signs that we often miss. I'll also explain why we sometimes have a gut instinct about somebody or something but choose to ignore it, and why ignoring your intuition is the last thing you want to do.

There's no denying that being scammed can hurt, and in more ways than one. It's not uncommon to experience a decline in confidence and self-esteem, as well as a sense of defeat following the ordeal. But with the right mindset and information, you can regain your confidence and bounce back greater than you were before, with even more resilience, too. The subsequent chapters provide steps you can take to realistically achieve all this, so read on!

Who Is This Book For?

This book is targeted at people who have experienced financial fraud and are struggling to see the light at the end of the tunnel. When you fall for a scam, especially one that costs you a lot of money like mine did, it's easy to beat yourself up and think there's no way back. That is why, in addition to educating you on how to recognize fraud, this book wants to inspire you by demonstrating the incredible resilience we humans possess without even realizing it. The stories and experiences described in this book mirror those of hundreds of thousands, if not millions of people around the world. By the end of this book, you will hopefully realize that you are not stupid for being duped. Scamming is literally their profession, and some scammers dedicate their whole lives to their craft, or even build entire organizations to aid them in their schemes. Realistically speaking, even though this book is primarily meant for those who have experienced being scammed, the information provided in the subsequent chapters can apply to everyone. So, if you'd like to learn how to avoid a scam in the future, then you should read on, too.

1

FRAGILITY TO LIES

During moments when it seems like all circumstances are conspiring against you, it is crucial to remember that the airplane overcomes the resistance of the wind during takeoff instead of depending on it.

– Henry Ford

The year of 2020 was undeniably one of the worst in recent memory. The Covid-19 pandemic was in full swing, and countries all around the world were forced to enact national lockdowns, which essentially confined people to their homes for months. The pandemic also precipitated a global economic downturn, which resulted in job losses, business closures and financial insecurity for many individuals and families.

Having said that, 2020 was a particularly trying year for me personally. Aside from the pandemic, my life felt like a house of cards, with the slightest breeze threatening to topple everything. The devastating news that seemed to keep coming in just exacerbated my complex emotional state, which was a mosaic of despair, grief and anxiety.

At the heart of this storm was the impending loss of my mother. In June of that year, I received the heartbreaking, stomach-churning news that my beloved mother had only a few days to live.

She was suffering from dementia, and her health had deteriorated to the point where doctors could no longer do anything for her.

Her once-vibrant spirit was now slowly dimming, and the looming inevitability of her passing cast a long shadow over our family. Each day felt like a fragile, treasured moment, yet the anticipation of her departure hung heavily in the air.

The social distancing restrictions enacted during the pandemic only added to the anguish of the situation. Mom was in a care facility at the time due to her advancing dementia, and it was a tragic twist of fate that prevented us, her three children, from being by her side during her dying moments.

As if the weight of my mother's impending loss wasn't enough to bear, life had another devastating curveball in store for us. My husband, my partner in life's journey, had just been handed a cruel and unwelcome diagnosis – a terminal illness. A seismic shock rattled the very foundation of our existence, leaving us both reeling in disbelief. The news hit us like a freight train, and it felt like the ground had shifted beneath our feet. We were suddenly thrust into uncharted territory, where the once-clear path of our future became a foggy maze of uncertainty. It left us grappling with profound questions about life, mortality and the fragility of our shared dreams.

Unsure of what the future held, I began looking for investments to help us in the future if necessary. And, in the midst of a difficult year, I discovered what I thought was the one ray of hope – an investment opportunity that promised to ensure my family's future. It was a syndicated investment in start-up enterprises.

A syndicated investment takes place when a group of people or organizations pool their resources to invest in a startup or early-stage company (Eeles, 2023). The process often starts with a lead investor, the person who takes the initiative to form an investing group, also known as a syndicate. The lead investor is usually an authority on the process because they have a lot of experience in investing, as well as a wealth of background information on the business in which they plan to invest.

The investors that become part of the syndicate typically have the choice of investing in each individual start-up opportunity that the lead investor presents. Each member of the syndicate pays a predetermined sum when the group agrees to fund a new business. By combining resources like this, more money can be invested, and down the line, more money can be made.

Investors consent to paying the lead investor a lead carry, which is a proportionate share of the proceeds, in return for their participation in the syndicate's investments. Essentially, the lead carry is a sort of remuneration for the lead investor's services.

To help visualize this, consider the following:

> Michelle, a well-known AngelList investor, is in charge of a syndicate that invests in start-up companies. Members of the syndicate may decide to put down a total of $200,000 in each of Michelle's start-ups, with the understanding that Michelle gets 15% of the earnings as lead carry.
>
> So, in one hypothetical investment situation, Michelle chooses to put $250,000 into a startup. She contributes $50,000 of her own money, with the syndicate members providing the remaining $200,000. In the event that the start-up investment is successful, the syndicate investors will get their original $200,000 back. Any leftover earnings will then be allocated as follows: Michelle receives 15% of the proceeds as her part of the profits, while the remaining 80% is distributed to the syndicate investors, and 5% is paid to AngelList Advisors, a subsidiary of AngelList that acts as a venture capital-exempt reporting adviser.

Equipped with this information, I was ecstatic! I couldn't believe that I had found, through online research an extraordinary investment opportunity like this, and considering the emotional state that I was in at the time, it allowed me to sleep more soundly at night.

As time went on, my excitement and confidence in this investment grew exponentially. I began to commit more substantial sums each month. The investment came with a personalized platform that provided daily updates, and I was elated to find that profits were consistently available for withdrawal at the end of each month. This inspired me to invest even more in the months that followed my initial returns. Luckily, while I was eager to recommend the opportunity to friends and family, I ultimately refrained from doing so. I am grateful I didn't, as I would have found it more challenging to cope with not only losing my own money, but also theirs.

During this period, I felt like a VIP. My investments came with exclusive invitations to events and thoughtful gifts from the lead investor. Life was good, and I reveled in the promise of financial success. Things went exceedingly well for around 19 months. However, as the calendar turned to January 2022, the rosy facade began to crumble, and I realized that things were not as they seemed.

As I reflect on what has happened in the last three years, it's clear that the fraudsters possessed charisma and cunning charm that lured me in when I was most vulnerable. On its face, their promise of financial freedom should have seemed too good to be true, but their powerful words were a carefully woven web that entangled my reason, leaving only my trust to give them. They guaranteed miraculous returns of 60%, which anyone would find enticing. On top of that, they promised bonuses, making the deal even more alluring. It was as if they held the keys to a hidden treasure trove of security and happiness, and they generously offered them to me alone. I was spellbound!

In every conversation we had, they seemed to understand my fears and desires intimately, making me believe they genuinely cared about my and my family's well-being. Their feigned empathy and concern became the glue that bound me to their illusion. Each word they uttered seemed tailor-made to alleviate my fears about investing and provide solutions to my deepest worries. I completely believed them when I heard such comments as:

> *"Amelia, please rest assured that your well-being is our top priority."*
>
> *"We acknowledge the challenges you have faced, and our dedication is to guarantee a stable and protected future for you."*
>
> *"You're not alone in this journey; we are here as your steadfast support system."*
>
> *"Don't hesitate to reach out if you need assistance or guidance."*
>
> *"We share your worries and fully understand them since so many of us have been where you are."*
>
> *"We are available by means of phone call, always willing to provide support and a sympathetic ear when needed."*

In my rational moments (and these were rare in 2020), I knew these comments and promises were too good to be true. But their words gained the most potency during those times of vulnerability when my emotions were raw, and my judgment was clouded by fear and uncertainty for the future. I was trapped in a paradox, aware of the danger, yet unable to escape their enchanting grasp.

During these moments, my intuition, a nagging voice of reason, would whisper warnings, casting doubt on the authenticity of their comments and promises. Deep down, I knew their words were too perfect and precisely tailored to what I wanted to hear. The alarms of skepticism would ring loudly, but the cacophony of my vulnerability quickly drowned them out.

It was in those raw, emotional moments when my guard was down, and my heart lay bare, that their words held the most power. Fear and uncertainty about the future cast a dense fog over my judgment, making it nearly impossible to see through the intricacies of their deceit. I found myself trapped in a paradoxical dance of awareness and helplessness.

As we delve deeper, you'll witness the intricate dance between their charm and my vulnerability, a dance that led me further down the rabbit hole of deception. But as the story unfolds, you'll also witness the awakening – the moment when I began to unravel the carefully woven web and find my way back to clarity and self-preservation. It's a tale of resilience in the face of cunning charm, a journey from enchantment to empowerment.

Emotional Triggers

What's comical about this whole fraud situation is that, amongst my friends and family, I am known to be the calm and sensible one. It just goes to show how all of us can fall prey to deceit under the right vulnerable circumstances.

I still remember the day I stumbled upon the scammer's advertisement. It was an especially long night, and when I couldn't get to sleep despite my best efforts, I got up and began surfing the web. It had only been about three weeks since my mother passed away, yet it still felt surreal. For the life of me, I couldn't wrap my head around the fact that my dear mother, the one constant in my life, was no longer here. Her passing, along with the prognosis given to my husband, served as a sobering reminder of the precarious nature of life. It felt as though, at any moment, something else that I held dear could be ripped away from me, and I wouldn't even see it coming.

As I sat there in the dark room, looking at my bright laptop screen, the words on the con artist's advertisement seemed like the only light in the depths of my hopelessness. They promised stability, financial security and a way to provide for my husband in his time of need. Their ad guaranteed extremely high returns on investments made in a startup syndicate, which was designed specifically for authorized investors like me.

I wondered, *What if this investment has the potential to bring me substantial cash so that I can find a doctor who can give my husband the greatest treatment possible, maybe even curing him?* After all, medical professionals have made mistakes or overlooked details when making diagnoses!

The testimonials of other families who had benefited from the startup syndicate also offered a glimmer of optimism. I wasn't completely sold just yet, but still curious, I clicked on the ad, and it took me to this professionally designed website that had a lot of images of successful businessmen and women. It appeared quite credible and had several touching testimonies. I was lured further into the scam when I encountered Mike, the purported "investment consultant," on the website's live chat.

Upon our first meeting, I couldn't help but feel a sense of calm and ease while chatting with him. He exuded an incredible amount of charisma and gave off the impression of being someone who genuinely cared about the predicament that I was in. He listened to everything I had to say without interruption and with great empathy.

I even told him about my recent struggles, losing my mom and receiving my husband's recent diagnosis. For some reason, I found it easier to confide in him than in my own husband and family. Maybe I was putting up a strong front for them, or maybe it was how the old saying goes: "Sometimes it's easier to open up to a stranger than a loved one." No matter what it could have been, there was no doubt that Mike had a unique way of expressing himself. He emanated an aura of authenticity and compassion that was hard to doubt.

To be entirely frank, however, I also just wanted to experience a feeling of hope and optimism. I so badly wanted to believe that I could do something in the present to help my family have a more stable future. I was essentially holding on to hope. Sure, maybe we couldn't save Mom or prevent my husband's diagnosis, but having a nest egg and some assets would give us a far better shot at a secure future.

After putting in a relatively small amount and seeing consistent monthly profits, I felt more secure in the firm. Soon after, I put every dime I had saved up and received as an inheritance from my mom into the investment, and as we already know, it completely blew up in my face.

RECOGNIZING VULNERABLE TIMES

Unfortunately, my experience is not unique. The practice of defrauding people out of their hard-earned money has become widespread and is now valued at billions of dollars.

In fact, according to new data, the Federal Trade Commission received 2.8 million allegations of fraud from customers in 2021 alone, accounting for a total loss of over $5.8 billion (Federal Trade Commission, 2022).

Anyone can fall victim to fraud. It doesn't matter what your age, salary, educational background or degree of financial literacy are. That being said, while it's true that there isn't a single demographic trait that makes someone more vulnerable to fraud than another, certain individuals are more predisposed to becoming victims. There are risk factors that increase your likelihood of falling for a con, such as:

- **Being stressed:** Stressful times in our lives may alter our reaction to deception. Situations that increase our susceptibility include losing a job, losing a loved one, being sick, getting divorced, having financial difficulties, having to care for others, feeling lonely and so forth. This is because our brain power is being diverted away from seeing fraud in favor of managing the stressor. Fraudsters may even search for such a life event and draw their victims' attention to it, further depleting their mental capacity.

- **Experiencing extreme emotions:** Strong emotions, whether positive or negative, increase our propensity to make poor judgments. To keep their victims off balance and make manipulation easier, scammers try to instill heightened emotions in them. This is because it is challenging for you to think clearly while your emotions are running high. Scammers skew people's judgment and force them to act impulsively by instilling feelings of urgency, anxiety or exhilaration. It makes no difference how smart or educated the victim is at this stage – the con artists have diminished their capacity for reason.
- **Being in a financial crunch:** This is a crucial element. People who are struggling financially or who are looking to make fast money are more susceptible to con artists who offer easy money or large investment returns. Under such conditions, the desperate attempt to better one's financial status might impair judgment and make one more vulnerable to scams.
- **Being unaware:** Scammers use cunning strategies to trick their victims, and a lot of people are just ignorant to the many kinds of scams. A lack of knowledge about new and emerging fraud tactics, including those utilizing blockchain and cryptocurrency, leaves people more open to attack. By remaining unaware, people unintentionally enhance their likelihood of being victims of fraud.
- **Lacking alertness:** The fast-paced nature of modern life and the abundance of distractions often lead to a decreased level of attentiveness, resulting in individuals unintentionally disregarding signs of caution or behaviors

that may be cause for concern. By not conducting thorough research, neglecting to verify the legitimacy of communications or offers, and not adequately safeguarding personal information, people can easily become susceptible to fraudulent activities.

- **Being socially isolated:** Usually, victims of fraud are more likely than the general population to experience social isolation or difficulties, even within their own families or relationships. Many are lonely, in need of assistance or experiencing a crisis, yet they lack support systems and are unsure of where to turn. Therefore, it should come as no surprise that elderly people are often a prime target for con artists, given their propensity for social isolation and reluctance to form new friendships. Furthermore, the Covid-19 epidemic increased the susceptibility of elderly people to financial abuse. Seniors are most commonly targeted for financial fraud when they are at their most vulnerable due to, for example, a health crisis or the recent loss of a loved one. Scammers often target their victims by gathering personal information from social media postings and obituaries. Some may also try to gain access to seniors' lives by taking advantage of the confidence they've placed in their social and support networks.

People who are socially isolated are also more likely to use the internet as a means of communication, rely on it as a means of escape, and initiate financial transactions and make purchases that they might have made in person but instead completed via the internet. Compared to those who are targeted by phone or email, lonely individuals who are approached by fraudsters via social media or a pop-up message on a website are more likely to interact with the scammer and lose more money. For some, loneliness is a driving factor in their search for love on the internet. Consequently, online relationship scams have grown more common as con artists are better able to hide their true identities behind the anonymity afforded by the web. It's important that you don't beat yourself too much if you've already fallen victim to a scam. Even though you may feel stupid for falling for it, it's important to understand that con artists are really effective manipulators who can fool anyone. Thus, being a victim of fraud does not always imply that you lack strength or intelligence.

Chapter 1 Summary

Amidst the trials the world faced during the tumultuous year of 2020, I took a moment to contemplate my own hardships. Specifically, I grappled with the imminent departure of my mother and the grave prognosis given to my partner. I found myself desiring stability and a bright future because of my overwhelming emotional turmoil, which unfortunately led me to fall for a scam. Without warning, I found myself completely ensnared in a deceptive investment scheme – a collective investment that guaranteed prosperity. Within this particular section, we explored the depths of emotional susceptibility that scammers manipulate, recollecting the way they were able to guide me toward a journey of deceit. We now know how stress, emotional extremes, financial challenges, a lack of alertness, distractions and social disconnectedness contribute to an individual's vulnerability to fraudulent activities.

2

GROOMING AND CAREFUL MANIPULATION

Each obstacle, hindrance and difficult situation holds the possibility for an equally or potentially greater positive outcome.

– Napoleon Hill

As my family faced the dual storms of my mother's loss and my husband's terminal illness, securing our future became an urgent priority. Everything seemed uncertain and fragile, and I was determined to find a way to provide for our loved ones, even in the face of adversity. In this chapter, we'll explore how personal loss, such as the departure of a loved one or a terminal illness diagnosis, can leave an indelible mark on our emotional psyche. In the tapestry of our lives, personal loss stands as one of the most profound and challenging experiences we may encounter. As I was to find out, a close second has to be financial loss, which brings with it a loss of identity and a feeling of deep shame. These are the moments when our emotional landscape becomes a labyrinth, with each twist and turn unveiling new triggers that can test our resilience.

Little did I know that my search for security for my family would lead me down a treacherous path. During this emotionally charged time, I unwittingly stumbled upon a group of scammers who were experts in exploiting emotionally vulnerable individuals.

When I first contacted the fraudsters back in June 2020, I didn't realize I was instantly being groomed and carefully manipulated. I was showered with attention, compliments and seeming kindness. It's like being wrapped in a warm, cozy blanket of deception. You begin to feel like you've found a true friend or a trustworthy advisor, unaware that the real agenda lies beneath the surface.

At first, their words sounded like a lifeline, a beacon of hope in my darkest hour. They painted a vivid picture of financial security and a brighter future, promising returns that seemed almost too good to be true. In my vulnerable state, I clung to their every word like a drowning person to a lifebuoy, desperate for a glimmer of hope.

I was unaware that I was on the brink of surrendering my entire financial future, making it the worst decision I could have ever made. Reflecting on that period, I still struggle to comprehend how I fell victim to it all. It feels as though it happened to someone else, not me, almost like I had an out-of-body experience.

It wasn't just me – the fraudsters appeared to be *everyone's* closest confidants. They amassed millions of dollars in investments while assuring clients they would never suffer a financial loss. Their charismatic charm captivated investors with astonishing pledges. They seemingly substantiated their claims by showcasing extraordinarily high monthly profit figures, which were undeniably thrilling. I soon found myself entangled in the intricate web of deceit.

The fraudsters lavished us with additional gifts throughout 2020 and 2021, owing to their substantial monthly profits. These included theater and sporting event tickets, tech gifts delivered by mail, gift vouchers for fine dining and high-end shopping experiences. We were treated like VIPs, and their generosity seemed to be unlimited. Little did we know that it was our money that funded these indulgences. These gifts were strategically employed to divert our attention from their fraudulent activities. Their plan was seemingly to keep us content, hoping that the money would continue to pour in – a strategy that ultimately proved successful.

As the web of deception tightened around me, I continued to believe every word they said. The fraudsters seemed to possess an uncanny ability to manipulate my emotions, exploiting my fears and insecurities to their advantage. It was a cruel irony that in my quest to secure my family's future, I had unwittingly become a victim of those who sought to exploit my vulnerability.

I realize now that it was a disorienting experience to be under the fraudster's spell. The gradual erosion of my skepticism and my unwavering trust in their false promises were very real. In our most vulnerable moments, we can be led to believe in the unbelievable, falling prey to the artful deception of those who prey on our emotions.

Looking back, in 2020, I was a prime target for scammers and fraudsters. I was acting irrationally and making impulsive decisions, which clouded my judgment and caused me to slide down the slippery slope of vulnerability. Living in a reactive mode, as I was, felt like enduring a constant barrage of emotional fireworks. At the same time, I felt like a tightly coiled spring, ready to snap at the slightest touch.

So, when the fraudsters delivered their well-rehearsed pitch, I was ripe for the taking because my emotional triggers were in full swing. Fraudsters excel at diversion, and when you're reacting impulsively, your ability to spot red flags disappears. In my case, that too-good-to-be-true investment opportunity appeared to be a once-in-a-lifetime chance, and I disregarded the glaring warning signs.

Looking back, I now understand how my fraudsters established trust with me. They frequently created a sense of urgency or fear, pushing me to invest more money with the allure of extraordinary rewards. The feeling that one has to act immediately or they'll miss out will prompt them to act hastily without critically evaluating the situation, and that's precisely what I was doing.

The scammers began with innocuous, small requests to build my trust. Once I complied, they gradually escalated to larger and more frequent demands for money. Meanwhile, they consistently showered me with the aforementioned gifts and invitations to exclusive events, all designed to keep me captivated and enticed.

My fraudsters possessed a remarkable talent for forging personal connections with us, the victims. They engaged in amicable conversations, inquired about my wellbeing and my family's welfare, and even divulged personal details about themselves, telling me about their families, hobbies and so on. This craftily constructed a false sense of friendship and trust. These were not amateurs but seasoned experts who had been defrauding people for decades, often adopting various disguises.

On that note, these fraudsters absorbed valuable lessons from their prior endeavors, and they had numerous attempts under their belts. They continuously adapted their tactics based on what yielded results and what did not. Each scheme was akin to a learning experience, allowing them to refine their approach.

And they had far too long to perfect their scam. This particular fraudulent empire was built by a mother and her partner while her sons were in their formative years. As they came of age, the boys joined their mother in this successful enterprise. Even though my case is on the verge of going to court now, it's astonishing that it took two decades to bring them to justice.

As I've said, my fraudsters were remarkably adept at harnessing psychological triggers to manipulate me. They skillfully employed tactics rooted in scarcity and reciprocity. In addition, they spun tales of their own tragedies to build a sense of rapport, and it worked. They were experts at exploiting various emotions, including fear, greed, curiosity and trust. These emotions were deftly manipulated to steer me toward specific actions, generating a palpable sense of pressure.

These tactics induced a feeling of pressure and compelled quick decision-making. All of this unfolded when I was already navigating an emotional rollercoaster within my family, making me particularly vulnerable to their manipulative tactics.

I've come to realize that successful fraudsters are among the most adept psychologists, possessing a profound understanding of human psychology. My fraudsters undoubtedly embodied this description. One of their paramount skills was their ability to cultivate trust with me swiftly, achieved through frequent, amiable conversations, sharing personal anecdotes and mirroring the conduct of trustworthy individuals.

Being duped doesn't mean you're naïve; rather, it shows how crafty the people who commit fraud are.

Establishing Trust

At first, the con artists lavished me with attention and assured me of a prosperous future, just like they had done with all their many previous victims. The more I conversed with Mike, the more I began to like him. He presented himself as a financial advisor, so our initial conversations were about our respective financial goals and concerns.

After hearing my story, he shared that he had gone through something similar to me, but instead of his mother passing away unexpectedly, it was his dad. He also shared that during that time, his mom, who resided in an old-age home, was gravely ill, and the death of his dad (who had been her husband for more than 40 years) only worsened her condition.

Mike told me that, as this all happened, he still worked as a financial advisor, but he was at a loss for what to do next. So, he decided to invest most of his life savings into a start-up company, and it turned out to be well worth the risk.

Before he knew it, his investment had yielded a very respectable return, allowing him to support his family and provide better care for his mother. Hearing this made my day. I felt like we were in the same boat and that he, more than anyone else, was able to get where I was coming from. Little did I know that this was just one of the many tactics that scammers employ to gain the trust of their victims.

The reason that Mike was more than eager to lend a listening ear is because con artists use this deeply personal information to gain your trust. In fact, scammers love to get their victims to talk as much as possible so they can learn more about you – and then use it to their advantage.

While conducting my research for this book, I had the opportunity to interview an ex-telemarketing scammer named Josh, and he told me that the key to pulling off a good con is appealing to the victim's desires. In other words, what can the scammer present to the target that will entice them to forsake logical thinking in pursuit of an illusory dream?

Asking someone directly is the most effective approach to uncovering their desires. He said that victims tend to answer a lot of questions rather than ask them. He went on to say that potential victims don't question whether or not the deal is legitimate, but rather focus on how to profit from it. "Deep down, the person being swindled unconsciously wants the scammer to inflate their ego and sense of self to the point where they are willing to ignore all warnings and go for it anyhow," he said. To be successful, a scammer must possess exceptional acting skills and be an attentive listener.

Over the course of my online conversations with my scammer, Mike, he increasingly opened up about his life outside of work. Our talks covered a wide range of topics, from our common interests to our hopes for the future. We would even crack jokes with each other; he and his co-conspirators always treated me with the utmost respect.

In no time at all, I found myself eagerly anticipating our next conversation and quickly began to view him as a genuine friend.

He eventually suggested we get together in person to go over the specifics of this rare investment opportunity, and I was game. I was both excited and a bit apprehensive about the prospect. Sure, I had grown to like and trust Mike throughout the few weeks we had been talking, but the idea of meeting someone who I had only known online was a significant step.

One night, after much back and forth, we decided to meet at a fancy restaurant in the city center. The evening was meticulously planned, and the mood was upscale and exclusive, appropriate for the big investment deal we were about to talk about. When I arrived, Mike was already there with a female colleague of his. When they saw me walking toward them, he stood up and extended a strong handshake as he welcomed me. His grin was instantly endearing, and he greeted me with the warmest welcome I've ever received. He then introduced me to his female coworker, whom he simply called "Angela," who greeted me with the same warmth and charm. Now that I think about it, Angela was probably just there to make the farce seem more legitimate and put me at ease. Mike and Angela both looked very professional and had an air of achievement about them.

They were clearly masters of their craft because one of the most important things in the conman handbook is to look at the part. When someone looks the part, we're more likely to take them seriously because they create a sense of credibility and trustworthiness. So, for example, if we see an attractive person who's also well dressed and well spoken, we're more likely to attribute other positive attributes to them – for example, assuming that they're smart, too – all without even knowing them very well.

As our night progressed, the conversations flowed effortlessly, and as we dined, Mike presented a well- rehearsed pitch for the investment opportunity. It was accompanied by eye-catching statistics and graphs that seemed to corroborate the prospect of high profits. He appeared to be quite sure of himself and his knowledge of the subject matter as he delivered his remarks.

Mike wasn't just taking advantage of the halo effect in this situation, but also expert bias. Expert bias, also known as authority bias, occurs when people blindly accept the ideas, techniques and recommendations of a perceived expert without doing independent research or drawing their own conclusions (The Knowledge, 2022). In other words, when information comes from someone we see as an expert, we are more inclined to take it seriously.

By the time our evening was coming to a close, I started to feel a stronger emotional connection to Mike. His attentiveness to my financial concerns and his shared vulnerabilities had created an unspoken bond of trust. He even advised me not to jump straight into the investment, even though he felt that it was my best option at the moment. He told me to take a few days to think about it and get back to them.

I agreed, and as I left the restaurant that evening, I did so with a sense of exhilaration about the investment and the knowledge that I had discovered a friend who actually cared about me and my family's wellbeing.

We swapped numbers, and over the next several days, I noticed a shift in the scammers' approach to trying to win me over completely. Whereas before they would shower me with compliments and kind gestures, they had now started to position themselves as guardians of my financial future. They would still compliment me, yes, but now they created this false sense of urgency. They told me that something unexpected had happened, so the perfect time to invest my money and reach the financial goals I'd outlined had just presented itself. Not wanting to miss out on this opportunity that seemed once in a lifetime, I poured the money in.

Mike suggested a rather moderate investment, so I didn't put in the whole $500,000 right away. This is another common tactic used by con artists, and I call it the small-step method. Scammers will ask you for a small amount, further build your trust, and then gradually increase the amount they take.

The phenomenon of online romance scams is a good example of this point of view in action. The victim of such a con is often encouraged to send ever-increasing sums of money as the relationship develops. Not too long ago, I met a man who had started chatting online with a stunning Ukrainian model. They soon began dating, and he invited her to come visit him in the United States. She said that she hardly had any cash and was having trouble making ends meet, much less afford a plane ticket to the United States. He was already head over heels in love with her at that point, so he promised to send her money for her rent and an airline ticket. She then explained that she was in danger, and that the embassy required her to pay for both the outbound and inbound flights as well as lodging before leaving, so he wired her an extra $5,000. She, as you may have guessed, never bought the ticket to come see him and continued coming up with excuses, and he, as you may have also guessed, kept giving her money. In the end, he sent $100,000 before the scam was exposed, and he was devastated.

Because, in my case, it wasn't a romance scam, the scammers switched things up a bit. To keep me sending in the dough, they cleverly made sure that I had good returns for those first couple of months. This made me have more confidence and trust in the investment, so I eventually saw it as a safe bet. I poured out all my money, which is what they wanted all along – to bleed me out for as much as they could until I had nothing left.

The Craft of Deceit

Whether it be in the name of love, war, politics or plain old fraud, one thing is certain: Throughout all of history, humans have consistently engaged in the skillful craft of deceit. Those who fall prey to scams don't give in to the deception because they're gullible, have an excessive desire for gain or are stupid. The majority of the time, it's not a character flaw, but rather a frame of mind that's to blame.

When we are feeling down and alone, our defenses are down, and we are more susceptible to being duped. When we're down and out, we're more likely to believe the kind stranger who appears out of the blue with simple solutions, despite our better judgment telling us that it's too good to be true.

It's astonishing how easily I, or anybody else, can be fooled. In fact, your chances of being duped increase the more certain you are that you can't be. During my interviews with various con artists for this book, I was often startled by how normal many of them came across. It's not as if you could just look at them and immediately conclude, "Ah, this person is an obvious habitual liar, sociopath and overall wicked human being." Many of them look like just your average Joe – nothing special about them at all. But of course, maintaining an air of normality is an integral part of the game. The so-called "dark triad" characteristics of narcissism, psychopathy and Machiavellianism are present in the majority of con artists' psychological profiles (*Psychology Today*, 2019). The nefarious characteristics that define each of these individuals are shared among them all.

Nevertheless, it is important to note that one's character is not the sole determinant of being a swindler. Many individuals who possess traits associated with the dark triad do not pursue careers as con artists. Some choose to pursue careers in various fields, such as medicine, military service, sales and so on. On the other hand, many others who don't necessarily possess the dark triad of traits end up in the con business due to financial necessity. But almost without exception, con artists have an uncanny knack for reading people. These are skills that can be used in many different contexts as well. Even though con artists are generally scumbags, one cannot help but revere their ingenuity at times.

While it's important not to lose sight of the fact that these are horrible individuals whose actions have lasting consequences, it's hard to deny that they're very skilled at what they do. The label "con artist" perfectly captures the nature of the profession. These are genuine artists who demonstrate an unwavering commitment to honing their skills. This is precisely the reason why all skilled deceivers begin by cultivating a bond with you.

It is widely understood that once we develop a liking for someone, it becomes increasingly challenging to detect their dishonesty due to our inherent subjectivity. They are counting on our being too invested in the relationship to see through their dishonesty. Plus, fraudsters are usually highly intelligent individuals who have figured out that the quickest approach to winning someone over is to act similarly to them.

It's human nature to gravitate toward those who are similar to you and share your interests. Scammers capitalize on our need for familiarity by preying on traits about us that are readily obvious. For example, if they find out that you are from Cleveland, they may say something like, "Oh, the Cleveland Browns are doing well this year," just to see if you're a football fan. And, if indeed you are, they'll steer the conversation in that direction, resulting in an unexpected connection as you both express your mutual passion for the sport of football.

This is the point where we begin to think, *"Hmm, this person cannot possibly be malicious; they exude such a remarkable aura."* Then, when you least expect it, they make an attempt to sell you a product or service, but not as a pushy salesman would, but rather as a close companion. This is exactly the same strategy that Mike used on me when he was sharing his "similar" financial and personal woes with me. So, if a friendship develops quickly and on a very superficial basis and then a request follows, this might be a red flag that the request is not what it seems to be.

In contrast to the "small step" method, which requires breaking things down into bite size chunks, there is also something known as the "door in the face" method. For example, a con artist may approach you and say, "Hey, I know we haven't known each other for very long, but can I ask you to run an errand for me tomorrow during rush hour?"

You would most likely respond with a hard "no" and maybe even question the rationality of the person making the request. This is understandable, considering it will require a significant portion of your time.

The scammer will probably respond with something like, "Oh, my apologies. I realize now that it's a significant inconvenience. There is no need to fret over it. I completely understand."

And then, after a few weeks have passed, they'll contact you again, this time to ask, "Hey, would you be willing to retrieve a box for me from the post office at 2 p.m. tomorrow? I'm afraid I won't be able to make it since I'll be super busy at that time."

Even though this is still a substantial request, you're probably going to respond with a yes. That's because you're probably still grappling with feelings of guilt from your initial refusal, despite the scammer's reassurance that it was inconsequential and they completely empathized with your decision. You still feel the effects of your past transgressions.

You'll feel so bad about saying no the first time that you'll give in.

That's why it's called the "door in the face" strategy: They essentially have to get you to slam the door in their face first, as doing so makes you feel horrible, and nobody likes to think of themselves as a bad person. It's a strategy that plays on our vulnerabilities as humans by manipulating our feelings and how we see ourselves.

All of us want that warm, fuzzy feeling of doing good. Con artists are aware of this, and they prey on it by convincing us to do things that will make us feel good about ourselves. Alternatively, forcing us into circumstances where saying no would make us seem like bad people, which is a self-image we don't want to have.

Con artists are also very skilled at reading the emotions of others around them. They are so perceptive that you may be unwittingly giving up all sorts of hints without realizing it. This is why they may seem clairvoyant at times, when, in fact, you're probably just giving them everything they need to go on. Their auras only seem mystical because the majority of us are bad listeners.

Consider the case of Victor Lustig, one of the most infamous con artists of the 20th century. Lustig achieved a remarkable feat by successfully selling the Eiffel Tower not once, but twice. Surprisingly, his actions went unreported on both occasions. The purchasers of the tower were so ashamed of being deceived that they chose to remain silent, allowing Lustig to execute his scheme twice without facing any consequences. This extraordinary tale of his exploits has been preserved for posterity.

He ended up writing a book called *The Ten Commandments of the Con Artist*, wherein he highlights a crucial principle: A successful swindler is not defined by their eloquence, but rather by their attentive listening skills. And, in my opinion, that provides you with all the necessary information. Scammers are individuals who genuinely pay attention. When you speak, they listen to what you say. They maintain a high level of focus. We non-con artists don't do that.

Usually, we don't pay much attention to the response when we ask a question. Our focus tends to be on ourselves rather than on the other person, resulting in us overlooking those nonverbal cues. Motivation is a factor that improves our ability to read other people. When we're feeling motivated, it's much easier to take in what other people are saying. It compels us to pay attention. Con artists have an incentive to pay attention since doing so is crucial to their success – they need to have a good read on you if they want to make a sale. Unfortunately, most of us lack such drive, so we fail to notice the clues before it's too late. Failing to notice these clues can allow farudulant activities to escalate, leading to significant financial damage before we even realise what's happening.

Chapter 2 Summary

In this chapter, I detailed the ordeal I went through at the hands of a gang of con artists who were adept at grooming and manipulating victims. I discussed the impact of my mother's departure and my husband's diagnosis on my emotional state, which left me feeling exposed and defenseless. At that moment, my mental state was clouded, and I felt an overwhelming need to find solace in the idea that there existed an action I could take to create a chain of positive consequences. We observed the scammers' cunning manipulation of my susceptibility through their excessive flattery, attention and deceptive acts of kindness. I was assured of a stable financial future and substantial profits, with impressive monthly returns and extravagant gifts funded using my own funds.

I also considered my vulnerability in a wider context, shedding light on the cunning tactics employed by scammers who skillfully manipulate psychological cues, such as time pressure, anxiety and reliance. The fraudsters, pretending to be reliable consultants, slowly increase their demands for funds by employing strategies that disarm us and build our trust, ultimately encouraging us to make decisions we normally wouldn't.

3

THE INVESTMENT FRAUD

It is impossible to step into the same river twice because it is different each time and the person is also different each time.

– Heraclitus

I had a history of making investments, but my previous experiences were markedly different from my unfortunate encounter with fraud. In the past, my investments were characterized by a strong foundation of trust and familiarity. I was what is typically referred to as a sophisticated investor, investing in companies, shares and syndicates with relative success. In the past, I only ever invested with people I knew and trusted implicitly, involving people who had established credibility and reliability over time. I felt comfortable investing because I had a deep trust in those I was dealing with, providing emotional security.

At times, we experienced minor setbacks where we incurred losses, but for the most part, our investments yielded substantial profits. These investments weren't characterized by overnight success but followed a gradual trajectory over several years. It was certainly not a "get rich quick" investment and demanded patience as a fundamental virtue. I felt at ease with this investment strategy, which proved highly effective, ultimately providing substantial financial benefits for my family.

Due to my past positive investment experiences, I had confidence in my judgment and decision-making abilities. This confidence further reinforced my willingness to explore investment opportunities in 2020 despite going through challenging times. During my previous investment ventures, I was always in an emotionally stable state. The stress, fear and vulnerability I felt when I became a victim of fraud did not influence my decisions.

Trust, familiarity and sound judgment were hallmarks of my prior investment history. However, as I've said in the first two chapters, my emotional vulnerability during a challenging period and the scammer's manipulative tactics led me to invest in a fraudulent scheme. This unfortunate turn of events serves as a reminder of how important it is to remain vigilant, even when dealing with investment opportunities that seem familiar or come from seemingly trustworthy sources, especially during emotionally trying times.

Because of the personal challenges I was going through, my investment strategy suddenly shifted in June 2020. I became irrational, and a pressing sense of urgency overcame me, compelling me to believe that I needed immediate access to funds. As a result of the panic that followed, I became illogical in my search for new investment opportunities.

Throughout 2020 and 2021, my confidence in my new investment soared to new heights. I was so convinced that I had struck gold that I ceased investing elsewhere, firmly believing that the fraudulent scheme would yield more significant and faster returns.

The investment fraud to which I gave my savings, involving a syndicate investing in startup companies, was tempting for several reasons. Financial aspirations, emotional vulnerability, trust in the syndicate's members and the allure of high returns all contributed to the temptation to invest in a startup syndicate.

The pitfall that eventually came with the fraud was the revelation that the entire investment opportunity was a carefully crafted deception. When I discovered the scheme's true nature, it had devastating consequences for me. The scam's most immediate and tangible impact was the significant financial loss. I had invested my hard-earned money and inheritance, which totaled $500,000, hoping for financial security and stability, but instead, I saw my savings vanish into the hands of fraudsters. Discovering that they had deceived and manipulated me took a severe emotional toll. It deepened the emotional turmoil I was experiencing due to my mother's passing and my husband's health deterioration. The sense of betrayal and helplessness only added to my emotional burden. Fraud can significantly strain relationships, as victims often grapple with self-blame and embarrassment for falling victim to deception. In my case, I was fortunate to have the unwavering support of my husband, family and friends. They rallied around me during this challenging time, providing invaluable emotional support and understanding, which helped alleviate some of the burden of shame and self-blame.

The aftermath of being defrauded can leave enduring psychological effects, including heightened anxiety, depression and a pervasive sense of vulnerability – challenges I encountered. Despite my longstanding interest in self-development, I initially struggled to employ the coping tips and techniques I had amassed over the years. The shock of the situation, coupled with overwhelming anxiety, insomnia and profound exhaustion, left me with little more than the ability to survive day to day. Emotionally, physically and mentally, I was burnt out. Eventually, I took the critical step of seeking therapy and counseling to address the trauma and work toward regaining my emotional well- being. This decision undoubtedly played a pivotal role in my recovery journey.

Navigating the aftermath of a fraud can be an arduous journey. Still, it's essential for victims like me to seek support, both emotionally and legally, to recover as best as possible. It is a stark reminder of the importance of staying vigilant, informed and cautious in financial dealings, and recognizing the signs of potential scams to prevent such devastating consequences.

In January 2022, I received a message that shattered my world: All the money I had invested, a substantial $500,000, was supposedly locked in a digital wallet, with the password irretrievably lost. The shock was so overwhelming that I felt physically sick. Upon receiving this devastating news, a wave of emotions washed over me: doubt, confusion, and a profound sense of disbelief. I began to question the legitimacy of the investment syndicate and the integrity of its claims. For the next six months, I clung to a state of denial, desperately hoping that the fraudsters' promises of repayment were truthful. I simply could not accept that all my money had vanished. Denial can be a potent psychological defense mechanism that shields individuals from the painful reality of being scammed.

Throughout this period, I maintained communication with the fraudsters, who used manipulative tactics to convince me that my money would be returned. They provided excuses, explanations and false reassurances to maintain my trust. As time elapsed and the promised repayments failed to materialize, the weight of reality began to crush me. I found myself torn between my desire to believe in the fraudsters' promises and the mounting evidence that I had been deceived.

The turning point arrived when the scammers abruptly cut off all contact. After stringing me along with false hopes, this action removed any lingering doubts about the fraudulent nature of the scheme. It was then that I was forced to confront the painful truth: I had indeed fallen victim to a fraud. The emotional toll of this realization was profound as I grappled with overwhelming feelings of anger, betrayal and regret.

In response to the scammers' disappearance and my acceptance of the scam, I eventually took action by reporting the fraudulent scheme to the relevant authorities and agencies, seeking assistance in addressing the situation. However, it took a few weeks as I struggled to come to terms with what had transpired. My journey from initial suspicion to eventual acceptance of the scam was undeniably emotionally challenging. It became even more difficult as a result of my protracted state of denial and the scammers' dishonest methods. This story is a stark reminder of the importance of early recognition and reporting suspicious financial transactions to prevent falling victim to scams and frauds.

Unbeknownst to you, fraud exposes latent reserves of inner fortitude and resilience.

Effective Decision-Making

The efficacy of scams lies in their ability to mimic authenticity, thereby ensnaring unsuspecting individuals during moments of vulnerability and unpreparedness. Fraudsters are very good at using new technologies, limited-time products or services, and important events to make up plausible stories that trick people into giving them their personal information or money. That's why you should always take your time to weigh the pros and cons before acting on something as significant as transferring money to someone you don't know very well.

Scammers depend on their victims missing obvious red flags, so they'll try to hurry you up by stressing the urgency of the situation. After all, most cons adhere to very standard narrative structures. This happens because con artists are smart enough to understand what approaches are most likely to succeed in defrauding their targets.

As a first step, con artists will attempt to get some kind of emotional response out of you, usually fear. A common tactic is to claim that a family member has been arrested and urgently needs your financial assistance to get out of police custody. Secondly, con artists will pressure you to take action immediately. The longer you give yourself to process what's going on, the less likely you are to end up a victim.

Similar to how fraudsters employ familiar tactics, such as instilling fear and inducing panic, they also tend to recycle the same fraudulent schemes repeatedly. By familiarizing yourself with the various types of prevalent fraudulent schemes, you can enhance your ability to recognize and steer clear of them. Cons may happen anywhere: on the internet, over the phone, via the mail or even face-to-face. Some of the most frequently encountered fraudulent schemes are:

- **Charity scams** occur when individuals approach you claiming to be raising funds for a noble cause. In actuality, when you contribute funds, the fraudsters retain the monetary resources exclusively for their own benefit.
- **Prepayment scams** require an advance payment of a nominal fee, which then entitles the recipient to an investment opportunity or the chance to win the lottery. They'll find out later, of course, that the investment or lottery does not exist.
- **Phantom debt scams** begin when people reach out to you under false pretenses, posing as debt collectors. There might be instances where people try to intimidate you by claiming that you owe debts that you don't actually have.
- **Internal Revenue Service (IRS) scams** occur when individuals falsely claim that you have outstanding tax liabilities or request your personal details under the guise of verifying the accuracy of your tax filings. These individuals make attempts to acquire both financial resources and personal data with the intention of perpetrating identity theft.

There is often a great deal of confusion surrounding the true definition of a scam. A fraudulent act does not involve an individual infiltrating your computer, smartphone or bank account with the intention of pilfering from you. Similarly, it does not encompass the act of purchasing an item that ultimately proves to be subpar in quality or paying an excessive amount for an item.

A genuine scam occurs when a person tricks you into divulging personal or financial details with the intention of stealing from you. The con artists behind scams are usually well-organized and savvy about how to avoid detection. Hence, it is advisable to exercise caution and refrain from providing any financial resources or personal details to others if you harbor even the slightest hint of doubt. Con artists often seem to want to aid you before asking for personal information. They'll pose as representatives from reputable institutions, such as law enforcement, your bank, the federal government or a fraud protection agency.

In addition, you shouldn't always take things at face value. It never hurts to wonder whether a call or message could be phony. Also, never open an attachment or click on a link in an email. If you need to get in touch with a company or government agency, your best bet is to use the information provided there or in their official applications. If you have any doubts, it is best to decline, end the call or remove the message.

What to Look for in a Scammer

At their core, individuals who engage in fraudulent activities are skilled in the art of deception, trickery and deceit. These individuals tend to possess an inherent inclination toward dishonesty and exploitation. Nonetheless, pinpointing these qualities is a skill that can be acquired and honed over time. With practice, one can cultivate the ability to detect it and cultivate a sense of intuition for it. Thus, I'll lay out a laundry list of clues that can help you begin to identify this.

So, to begin, you should be wary of anyone who makes numerous or outlandish promises to you and has a propensity for boasting and exaggeration. Exercise extreme caution when encountering people who guarantee rapid wealth accumulation or a surge in business opportunities.

It is important to remain vigilant about certain indicators that may raise concerns. For instance, if an individual displays an excessive level of charm, possesses exceptional storytelling abilities, exhibits a highly outgoing nature, exudes a captivating aura, consistently dresses in a sophisticated manner and consistently demonstrates an overly pleasant demeanor, these could all potentially serve as cautionary signs.

Obviously, not everybody who is extroverted, literate and well-dressed is out to defraud you. A lot of the time, it's just who they are and the way they choose to express themselves. However, it's still crucial to exercise caution in relation to this warning sign because con artists sometimes use charm and good communication as a ruse. They usually use their eloquence and captivating mannerisms so that their victim develops a fondness for them and therefore lowers their defenses.

The scammer's ability to captivate with their storytelling prowess, humor, sophistication, style and charisma can be so remarkable that it becomes way too easy to overlook the true essence of the potential "business opportunity." When you fail to ask pertinent questions, you put yourself in a vulnerable position. It's safe to assume that whatever looks way too good to be true really is.

It is equally important to develop the skill of identifying individuals with a lack of intellectual integrity. Maintaining your intellectual integrity entails acting in accordance with your best judgment of the truth. A lot of con artists lack this trait, so when you come across someone whose actions don't match what they say is true, it's best to be on high alert because being dishonest isn't a big deal to them. When you show disregard for the truth, it grants you the freedom to partake in deceit and dishonesty. Therefore, you should ascertain whether or not the individual or organization you are working with places a premium on honesty.

Emotional manipulation is another warning sign to keep an eye out for. Fear, desire, ambition, anger, laziness, desperation and love are all emotions that can be employed to create a barrier between you and your financial resources.

If someone is offering you a speedy path to riches, be skeptical. Con artists understand that most people would prefer to take the easy route – if there ever was one. This is essentially a scammer preying on your idleness. Most people don't want to put in the time and effort required to make a lot of money, just like many of us don't want to put in the work at the gym but still want the results.

The con artist's main product is the so-called "quick fix", which, unfortunately, proves to be ineffective in most cases. These shortcuts often lead to disappointment, and in some instances, they can even have detrimental effects on your wellbeing, finances and overall contentment. Be cautious when something appears extremely simple or quick, as it often turns out to be false. Consider the actual expense of what they propose and trust your gut instinct when making a decision.

A lot of us fall victim to scams in this manner because we fail to recognize the genuine value of achieving something. For example, if you're serious about becoming fit and losing weight, the first thing you'll have to ask yourself is, *"Just how much will it really cost me to maintain a healthy lifestyle?"* Success comes from making little, consistent changes to one's lifestyle, including exercising regularly and eating healthily. The same thing goes for financial freedom. Achieving financial success is neither a quick nor an inherently enjoyable journey.

Upon careful reflection, it becomes evident that achieving financial independence and establishing a passive income typically entails a substantial investment of time and hard work, and an unwavering commitment to acquiring knowledge pertaining to a specific subject or industry. Achieving significant results often requires a prolonged period of dedicated effort, during which the rewards gained from such endeavors can often amount to substantial wealth. It is rather illogical when an individual presents you with identical benefits in exchange for only half the duration of the effort. If an individual approaches you with a proposition to purchase a program promising the "keys to rapid wealth creation," it is advisable to steer clear.

To effectively protect yourself from falling victim to scams, it is necessary to adopt a proactive approach by conducting thorough inquiries and displaying a keen eye for detail. Don't be afraid to ask the salesperson so many questions that they start to become annoyed. Allow them to grow irritated and get all the information you want since it is in the specifics that issues and inconsistencies become apparent.

Finally, while looking into and evaluating such circumstances, you should ask yourself, *"Can this be sustained?"* In most instances, swindlers try to peddle a service or product that is blatantly impracticable. It's usually a case of taking a deeper look at what they are offering you. Most people lack awareness of sustainability; therefore, the next time you're contemplating doing business, making an investment, forming a partnership or anything else, always keep sustainability in mind. Consider if this is something you can continue in the long run since most con artists and fraudsters have extremely short-term thinking. Their focus is on quick gains, as they want to build a structure like a house of cards, which seems sturdy at first but will crumble when one of the cards is even slightly disturbed.

Strategies for Responding to a Recent Scam

If you find yourself caught in the unfortunate web of a scam, try not to jump into panic mode immediately. There are several proactive steps you can take to increase the likelihood of reclaiming your funds and restoring your peace of mind. They consist of the following:

VERIFY THE EXTENT OF YOUR INSURANCE POLICY

If you happen to have insurance coverage for identity theft, it is advisable to contact your provider as the first step in responding to a scam. The service provider will assist in safeguarding your accounts, detecting fraudulent activities and guiding you through the various stages of the recovery process. It is possible that your employer's insurance plan may provide coverage for you. Certain types of property insurance may provide coverage for lost or stolen personal belongings, including important documents, cash or credit cards.

TAKE IMMEDIATE ACTION TO EVALUATE THE COMPLETE EXTENT OF THE HARM

Fraudsters rely on the delay in your ability to identify the indications of deception. The longer you delay reporting the incident, the greater the opportunity for them to pilfer. Upon realizing that you have become the focus of attention, it is crucial to promptly commence the process of inspecting and recording any potential harm inflicted. Furthermore, in the event that you have enrolled in a credit-monitoring service, and they have notified you about the fraudulent activity, it is best to commence your investigation from that point. Next, you should thoroughly review your additional financial accounts for any signs of potentially fraudulent behavior. You also have the right to receive a complimentary credit report from each of the three main credit bureaus (Experian, Equifax, Transunion) so take advantage of that resource, too.

INFORM THE FINANCIAL INSTITUTIONS FROM WHICH YOU BORROW

Once you know the extent of the fraudulent activities, it is imperative that you take immediate action to safeguard your accounts by blocking the perpetrators' access. Begin by reaching out to your financial institution, such as your bank, credit card provider or any other relevant organizations that may have been affected, and inform them about the fraudulent activity. Your accounts will be terminated, and they will guide you through the subsequent procedures.

ESTABLISH NOTIFICATIONS FOR POTENTIAL FRAUDULENT ACTIVITY WITH THREE DIFFERENT AGENCIES

It is crucial to promptly inform the three primary credit reporting agencies about the fraudulent activity you have experienced. A fraud alert can be activated on your account as a precautionary measure to prevent people from fraudulently opening new accounts using your personal information. You can reach out to one of the three major credit bureaus that we just discussed, so they can add a fraud alert to your account. Fortunately, you only have to reach out to a single company, as they are legally obligated to notify the remaining parties about the fraudulent activity.

One option to consider is implementing a security freeze, which effectively restricts the sharing of your credit report with any external parties until it is removed. You also have the option to set up a preliminary warning for potential fraudulent activity on your credit file. With this in place, lenders must confirm your identity prior to granting approval for any new credit. The duration of this notification is one year unless you decide to remove it ahead of time. Lastly, you may consider setting up a prolonged deception warning. Once you have submitted your report to the Federal Trade Commission (FTC), it is possible to request an extended fraud alert that remains effective for an additional seven years past what you'd get with a preliminary warning. You have the option to remove all freezes and alerts without any cost at your convenience before the seven years are up.

PROTECT YOUR DIGITAL ACCOUNTS FROM THE RISK OF IDENTITY THEFT

Changing your password and locking your account are both prudent measures to take in the face of rising cybercrime. It is wise to use robust passwords that consist of at least eight characters. These passwords should include a combination of letters, numbers and symbols, as well as both lowercase and uppercase characters. Establish a reliable password-management system to effectively monitor and safeguard your passwords while also receiving timely notifications regarding any compromised accounts. Lastly, make sure to activate multi-factor authentication for every account that offers this feature. This may mean you'll log in with a password, and then verify it's you with a unique code sent to your phone or email address. Or, you might have to input the answer to a secret question you created when setting up your account. Some companies use fingerprint scanning for added security, too.

FILE A COMPLAINT WITH THE FEDERAL TRADE COMMISSION (FTC) REGARDING THE FRAUDULENT ACTIVITY AND IDENTITY THEFT

To report incidents of identity theft, you have the option of submitting your report to the Federal Trade Commission (FTC) through a designated website, identitytheft.gov. You will receive a certified document for identity theft, which can be utilized to challenge unauthorized charges and restore your credit score. After completing it, make sure to generate the sworn statement and retain a duplicate for your personal files. To ensure a thorough reporting process, it is essential to contact your credit card companies, financial institutions and local law enforcement regarding the crime.

SUBMIT A FORMAL COMPLAINT TO LAW ENFORCEMENT AUTHORITIES

On that note, after submitting an identity theft report to the FTC, various law enforcement agencies have the ability to retrieve and utilize it as part of their own investigations. There is a compelling rationale for taking action when you possess knowledge about the perpetrator of fraud or identity theft, or if you possess valuable information that could aid law enforcement in apprehending the individual responsible for the fraudulent activities. If you suspect that your identity was stolen and used to commit a crime, you should also submit a police complaint.

FILE A DISPUTE AGAINST FRAUDULENT PURCHASES AND BEGIN THE PROCESS OF REPAIRING YOUR CREDIT

After ensuring the safety of your personal information and online accounts, it becomes necessary to begin the process of rectifying the harm that was caused. Ensure that you reach out to the relevant organization involved in the fraudulent activity and provide them with the necessary documentation that can be used as evidence, such as your reports from the FTC and the police. Firstly, it is crucial to address any inaccuracies present on your credit report and challenge them accordingly. It is also important to take immediate action to close any recently opened accounts that have been fraudulently established under your name. Credit agencies must also take immediate action when discovering bogus accounts. Like many criminals, fraudsters often have a tendency to revisit the location where a crime took place. Therefore, if you have previously fallen victim to fraud, it is highly likely that they will try to target you once more.

Chapter 3 Summary

In this chapter, we looked at how I wasn't what you would call a "typical" fraud victim. Not only had I invested in other projects before, but I was also level-headed and respected when it came to the world of investing. Even so, I still found myself in the hands of scammers and went from making profitable investments to becoming a victim of a syndicate scam, resulting in a loss of $500,000. This part of the story serves as a clear demonstration that, irrespective of one's identity or standing, we all possess the potential to be deceived. This is especially true when we find ourselves in a desperate and vulnerable position. For me, emotional vulnerability during personal challenges led to impulsive decisions, which ultimately resulted in substantial financial setbacks and emotional distress. This section of the story describes how the shock of learning that the money was purportedly locked resulted in denial and misplaced optimism. This story shows how important therapy and mental support are for getting better.

4

KEEPING THE LIE ALIVE

Out of difficulties grow miracles.

– Jean de La Bruyère

My fraudsters were skilled at maintaining the illusion of a legitimate investment, using a range of tricks and tactics to cover up discrepancies and red flags. Some examples of what I experienced include a sophisticated website that mimicked the online presence of a legitimate financial business, alongside a portfolio of incredible profits. They used professional graphics, logos and content to make the websites appear genuine. They provided me with contact information of the person I was to deal with throughout, such as phone numbers, email addresses and WhatsApp groups that appeared legitimate. The fraudsters placed fake testimonials and reviews on their websites and in their promotional materials. These glowing recommendations were fabricated to give the impression of satisfied investors. I was presented with complex investment strategies and financial jargon to make the opportunity seem sophisticated and legitimate.

They also used technical-sounding terms to confuse and deter any of my questions. I received weekly, monthly and occasionally daily updates, reporting fabricated positive developments in the investment. These updates were designed to keep me engaged and hopeful, even when profits seemed to have dipped a little. When I asked questions or expressed concerns, the fraudsters diverted my attention by introducing new information or fabricating issues. This tactic made it difficult for me to focus on the red flags. When I asked about delayed or missing payments, the fraudsters gave excuses such as technical glitches, regulatory hurdles and bank errors. They even made partial payments to maintain the illusion of legitimacy. I was also discouraged more than once from seeking advice or opinions from trusted friends, family members or financial professionals.

By employing these tactics, fraudsters aim to create a convincing facade of legitimacy that obscures discrepancies and red flags. Consequently, I found it challenging to discern the truth amid the elaborate deception, making it crucial to exercise caution, conduct due diligence, and seek independent advice when considering my investment opportunity.

Now and then, I would catch glimpses of red flags. However, my obsession with the returns and the promise of a brighter future caused me to dismiss them all. I wasn't thinking rationally, but it didn't seem to matter at that moment. I believed I had discovered a foolproof formula to secure my future for a lifetime.

As we've discussed, recognizing early warning signs of potential financial fraud is crucial for safeguarding one's investments. However, these signs can often be subtle and easily overlooked, especially when trust, emotions and manipulative tactics come into play. Reflecting on my own experience, there were several red flags that I either missed or chose to ignore.

My fraudster avoided disclosing crucial details when asked, such as information about the types of investments, timeline and amounts invested. At the time, I placed too much trust in their verbal assurances and disregarded the absence of transparency. I dismissed minor inconsistencies and errors in their communications, being charmed and manipulated into accepting their explanations.

Recognizing these early warning signs demands vigilance, skepticism and a willingness to seek independent advice. Unfortunately, during the 19 months of my investment, I didn't exercise these precautions, which left me vulnerable to deception. Acknowledging these missed opportunities for scrutiny is a valuable step in preventing such scams in the future and encouraging others to remain vigilant when evaluating financial opportunities.

As the truth of the investment scam slowly unraveled, a complex mix of emotions flooded over me. These emotions were profoundly distressing and included the usual:

- **Feelings of anger and frustration** at having been deceived and defrauded
- **Betrayal and emotional hurt**, given the emotional connection I had developed with the fraudsters
- **Guilt and self-blame**, which is common but can be particularly harsh, and I found it challenging to comprehend how I could have been so trusting
- **Shame and embarrassment** about being taken advantage of and concerns about how others would perceive me
- **Fear of judgment** from friends, family and colleagues, adding to the emotional burden

Navigating these emotions can be an arduous journey, and seeking support and understanding from those who care about you is essential. Reaching out to professionals and support networks can also be instrumental in the healing process. In addition to the emotions mentioned earlier, the experience of being defrauded brought about a range of other intense feelings, including:

- **Anxiety**, a pervasive sense of unease and worry about the financial and emotional repercussions of the scam
- **Stress** from the burden of dealing with the aftermath of the fraud, including legal matters and financial losses

- **Regret**, wishing that different choices had been made and that the scam could have been avoided
- **Sorrow** for the financial losses and from the emotional toll inflicted by the fraud
- **Powerlessness** over the situation, particularly when dealing with the aftermath of the fraud
- **Vulnerability** from my heightened awareness of fraud, and a new distrust toward others
- **Despair** in the face of financial losses and emotional turmoil
- **Isolation** in the experience, as discussing being defrauded with others can be challenging
- **Withdrawal** from social and personal activities as a result of the emotional impact of the scam

These emotions collectively paint a vivid picture of the profound distress and turmoil that come with falling victim to fraud. Acknowledging and addressing these emotions as part of the healing and recovery process is essential. Seeking support from loved ones and professionals can be invaluable in coping with these feelings and moving forward.

My journey of coming to terms with the fact that I was defrauded was a painful and emotionally challenging process that unfolded in several stages:

- **Initial denial and disbelief:** When I first encountered signs that something might be wrong with the investment, such as the messages about lost passwords and locked digital wallets, this is when I experienced a sense of denial and disbelief.
- **Gradual suspicions:** Over time, as the promised returns failed to materialize and the fraudsters provided excuses and delays, my initial doubts evolved into more profound suspicions. I started researching online but also maintained regular contact with the fraudsters, as I was worried they could disappear.

- **Red flags found:** During my investigation, I found several red flags and inconsistencies in the information the fraudsters had provided. These red flags included companies being dissolved, fraudsters changing their online status and many discrepancies in the investment details.
- **Cutting off contact:** The turning point came when the fraudsters abruptly cut all contact. This abrupt disappearance shattered the illusion of trust and support that had been meticulously built.
- **Acceptance:** With the sudden loss of contact and the growing evidence of deception, I was forced to confront a painful reality – I had indeed been defrauded. This acceptance was accompanied by a wave of emotions, including anger, betrayal and regret.
- **Reporting the scam:** In response to the scammers' disappearance and my acceptance of the fraud, after several weeks, I took steps to report the fraudulent scheme to relevant authorities and agencies, as outlined in the previous chapter.
- **Seeking support and recovery:** Coming to terms with being defrauded was emotionally distressing, and I sought emotional support from friends and family. Later, I contacted support groups for more guidance on what I was going through. Eventually, I went into therapy and had counseling to help navigate the aftermath and cope with the psychological impact.
- **Rebuilding trust and moving forward:** This is an ongoing process, in both my financial dealings and interpersonal relationships. I took steps to regain my financial stability and became more vigilant about potential fraud. The journey of coming to terms with being defrauded is difficult, marked by a rollercoaster of emotions and the need for emotional and practical support. It is a stark reminder of the importance of staying vigilant, informed and cautious in financial dealings, and recognizing the signs of potential scams to prevent such devastating consequences.

Handling the shock and disappointment of discovering the full scope of deceit in a scam can be challenging and emotionally taxing. Here are some strategies I suggest to help cope with these emotions, as they helped me in my journey:

- **Allow yourself to feel** the shock, disappointment, anger and other emotions that arise. Acknowledge that having these feelings is normal when you've been deceived.
- **Ask for emotional support** from trusted individuals. Reach out to friends and family members who can offer emotional support and a listening ear. Sharing your experience with someone you trust can provide comfort.
- **Support groups** for scam victims offer a safe space to connect with others who have gone through similar experiences. Consider joining one.
- **Seek professional help.** Their expert guidance will allow you to process your emotions and develop coping strategies. They can help you navigate the psychological impact of the scam.
- **Avoid self-blame.** Understand that anyone can fall victim to scams, so it does not reflect on intelligence level or judgment. Scammers are skilled manipulators who prey on vulnerabilities.
- **Report the scam** to the appropriate authorities or agencies. Knowing that you've prevented the fraud from affecting others can provide a sense of empowerment.
- **Assess your financial situation** and develop a plan to recover as best as possible. Consult with a financial advisor if needed to create a financial recovery strategy.
- **Rebuild your financial security** over time. Set realistic financial goals and work toward them gradually.
- **Educate yourself about investment scams.** Learn to recognize red flags and protect yourself in the future.

- **Consider sharing your experience** to raise awareness about scams and help prevent others from falling victim.
- **Set boundaries** to protect your personal information and financial assets. Be cautious of unsolicited contact, especially from unknown sources.
- **Stay vigilant and remain cautious.** Continue to be vigilant when considering investment opportunities or engaging in financial transactions. Have faith in your intuition and carry out thorough research.
- **Make yourself a top priority.** Nurture both your physical and emotional health with the utmost dedication. Partake in endeavors that fill your heart with delight, tranquility and a sense of liberation from life's pressures.
- **Forgive yourself** for any decisions made in good faith that led to the scam. Understand that everyone makes mistakes, and this experience is a chance for growth. Show yourself the compassion you would give to others.
- **Consult legal experts and consider legal action.** Depending on the circumstances, consult with legal professionals to explore potential avenues for recovering lost funds or seeking justice. Coping with the shock and disappointment of a scam is a process that takes time. It's essential to be patient with yourself and seek the support you need to heal emotionally and, where possible, financially. Remember that you are not alone in facing such challenges, and there is hope for recovery and a brighter future.

Individuals who have been targeted by fraudulent activities are not simply passive victims, but rather tenacious fighters who overcome challenges and reconstruct their lives with unwavering determination.

Early Warning Signs

Investing always involves a certain level of uncertainty. However, assessing the degree of uncertainty can often be challenging. While your desire for profits and willingness to take risks play a role, making wise investment decisions also requires careful thought and study, as well as faith in both the salesperson and your instincts. Instances of investment fraud are quite prevalent, and although it can be challenging to identify, there are certain unmistakable indicators that might suggest an investment opportunity is not what it seems. Watch out for these warning signs before making investments:

SHADY PRACTICES BY BROKERS

Keep in mind that commission-based brokers aren't required to prioritize customer demands. A broker may be more likely to promote investments that cost more, seeing as they pay higher commissions than investments that pay lower commissions. Additionally, be wary of any marketing strategies they may attempt to implement and adopt a skeptical stance. Given that it's their job to sell, brokers who try to hype up an investment as an "upcoming sensation" or "gateway to prosperity" or act like they have "inside information" (which is against the law) should probably be avoided.

INABILITY TO WITHDRAW YOUR FUNDS

An investment is said to be liquid if it can be quickly and easily turned into cash. Consider the ease with which stock and bond investments may be converted into cash as an example of this. It is important to remember that larger assets, such as real estate, may need more time to be converted into cash. There are more serious implications to think about if you can't get your money whenever you want to from an investment. If there are hiccups while trying to withdraw money, it might be an indication of fraud. Conditions such as redemption periods for hedge funds, written agreements for partnership interests and other liquidity limits may interfere with your ability to withdraw cash at will. These restrictions, however, should be agreed upon before you make any investment decisions and only apply to certain types of investments, such as fixed-term instruments, like Certificates of Deposit (CD's).

If you're being encouraged to "reinvest" pledged payments with increased investment yields," tread carefully. This is a classic Ponzi scam approach.

LACK OF TRANSPARENCY

In the realm of investment, trust is built upon the foundation of transparency. When encountering an investment opportunity that lacks comprehensive details regarding its operations, underlying assets or the individuals involved, it's best to step back. Paperwork, financial records and an open operational framework are readily available in reliable investment opportunities. Feel free to inquire about any uncertainties and make sure to conduct thorough research to gain clarity on the destination of your funds.

SECRETIVE OR CONFIDENTIAL INVESTMENTS

This could potentially be the most apparent hint that something is amiss. By requesting that you maintain confidentiality regarding a transaction, fraudsters are able to stop loved ones and acquaintances from detecting the fraudulent scheme. Before making any drastic investments, be sure you've discussed the scheme with a reliable and trustworthy source first.

INVESTMENTS THAT REQUIRE YOU TO BORROW

A responsible salesperson will never encourage a client to use their entire life savings on a single investment. Instead, they should always ensure that they thoroughly discuss your previous investment background and level of comfort with risk prior to suggesting any investment opportunities. This crucial step in the salés process may be overlooked by a deceptive individual.

Furthermore, they should not request false or invented information on your application or your bank account number, or suggest borrowing funds, particularly from a retirement account, for investment purposes. Certain astute investors employ margin, which involves borrowing funds, to amplify the impact of their investment. However, only the most daring investors should attempt this.

EXCESSIVELY COMPLEX INVESTMENTS

It is wise to exercise caution when considering investment strategies that employ excessive jargon while simultaneously targeting smaller investors with a maximum initial investment limit of $100,000. Inexperienced investors may find themselves susceptible to fraud because they often neglect to conduct thorough research. Do not fall for the misconception that one's age, youthfulness or lack of financial experience hinders their ability to comprehend investments. Most importantly, don't put your money into something you do not fully understand – it's that simple.

UNREGISTERED OR UNREGULATED INVESTMENTS

Those just starting out shouldn't put their money in unregistered ventures, which are designed for individuals who meet the criteria of being "accredited investors," meaning they have sufficient wealth to withstand any potential losses. Investments that are not registered are not required to follow identical securities laws and regulations that safeguard individuals who invest in stocks or bonds that are publicly traded. Unless one possesses expertise in investing, it is advisable to focus on traditionally regulated securities. If you find yourself uncertain about the agent or company, it is advisable to seek verification from regulators. You should also make sure that investments have undergone proper verification by regulatory organizations like the Securities and Exchange Commission (SEC), a state securities regulator or the National Association of Securities Dealers.

UNUSUALLY HIGH RATES OF RETURN

In broad terms, it can be said that investments carrying greater potential for returns also tend to involve higher levels of risk. If an individual claims that an investment opportunity provides "assurance," meaning money put in will undoubtedly be returned to you, it would be prudent to express skepticism. Trends tend to vary over time, so an investment that consistently yields favorable results may seem too good to be true, as it is simply not feasible.

Never put your confidence in someone who guarantees a large return quickly. The primary feature of investment fraud is the attainment of returns that surpass the market average. It is the lure crafted to ensnare you.

Phrases such as "minimal risk," "negligible risk" or "assured outcome" are further signs of potential investment deception. The truth is that every financial plan has a weak spot, which means that "no risk" is not a real thing. The greater the assurance you receive, the more important it becomes to thoroughly evaluate the specific protections being offered. Respected investments offer investors a clear perspective on possible risks, enabling them to make informed decisions.

RESEMBLANCE TO A PYRAMID OR PONZI SCHEME

Exercise caution when dealing with investment schemes that depend on enlisting fresh investors in order to provide returns to previous investors. Both pyramid and Ponzi schemes are inherently unsustainable, leading to their eventual downfall and causing significant financial losses for numerous investors. Examine the investment's business model and revenue streams to verify that it is not functioning as a pyramid scheme.

Why We Disregard the Warning Signs

One perspective that I find compelling regarding the prevalence of falling for scams is the concept known as "optimism bias." This term describes the human propensity to downplay the possibility that they would become a victim of a scam. Unfortunately, this false sense of security often causes individuals to disregard red flags and take chances they otherwise would have avoided.

This particular cognitive bias has the potential to increase our susceptibility to scams, as it may result in us neglecting essential precautions or being less cautious when evaluating possible dangers. Consequently, it is possible for us to disregard the warning signs, under the assumption that our intelligence and knowledge make us immune to falling prey. I must admit, to some degree, that I also held this belief.

Given my track record of investing success, I never anticipated being a victim of investment fraud. People need to be cognizant of this tendency and take a more circumspect stance when weighing possibilities or deals.

REASONS WHY YOU SHOULD TRUST YOUR INSTINCTS

An intuition, premonition or instinct – no matter what term you prefer to use, the unexpected burst of understanding from within has the power to ignite a great deal of belief. The age-old saying tells you to "rely on your instincts," meaning you should trust these sensations, often as a means of remaining authentic to oneself.

Still, a substantial percentage of individuals, approximately 70 percent, tend to disregard their intuition when faced with financial matters, thereby increasing their susceptibility to fraudulent individuals. This is what the bank Barclays claims anyway, adding that purchase scams (which are when individuals buy things that never come or aren't as described) have increased by 70 percent year over year (Barclays, 2023).

Trusting your intuition can guide you toward the optimal route for your personal journey. However, you may ask whether you should place your faith in something you can't rationalize, like a gut instinct. I believe that you most certainly should. The brain and stomach are in constant, reciprocal communication. This phenomenon is commonly referred to as the brain-gut connection or axis, which is facilitated by an intricate network of countless nerves linking these two vital organs. The sensation in your gut, the one that's supported by scientific evidence, is frequently rooted in instinct and possesses the ability to ensure your safety in multiple respects.

So, following your intuition may shield you from the daily threats of fraud and scams that many people encounter. Intuitive instincts can elicit various sensations, similar to the bodily sensations linked to feelings of unease. On the other hand, alternative, more optimistic feelings may seem to validate your decision.

While intuition may be thought of as a quiet voice inside of you, it frequently makes itself known in more obvious ways, such as:

- A brief moment of lucidity
- Stiffness or tension throughout your body
- Goosebumps or tingling
- Fluttering in the stomach or queasiness
- A sinking feeling deep within your abdomen
- Sweaty palms or feet
- Persistent thoughts that revolve around a particular individual or circumstance
- Emotions of tranquility, security or joy (once you've reached a positive outcome)

Despite appearing to happen suddenly, intuition is not random, nor does it actually stem from your stomach. Abdominal discomfort can sometimes be a result of the connection between the brain and the stomach, as emotional experiences can have an impact on our digestive system. If someone is feeling anxious, scared or has a sense of impending disaster, they may also experience uneasiness, slight pains or an unsettled stomach.

WHEN SHOULD YOU GO WITH YOUR GUT?

Intuitive senses can manifest as tangible details rooted in keen observation and personal encounters. However, it's probably not a good idea to rely on them for everything. Here are a few examples of when going with your instinct is likely to pay off.

WHEN YOU ARE ABLE TO DISTINGUISH THEM FROM MERE HOPEFUL THOUGHTS

Wishful thinking occurs when a person desires a particular outcome with so much intensity that they start to convince themselves of its inevitability.

Imagine if you've harbored a long-standing desire to achieve financial success by making shrewd financial decisions, even though you've previously experienced the unfortunate consequences of a fraudulent financial scheme. If you retain that hopeful mindset and are given another chance to invest in a seemingly profitable venture, you will persuade yourself that the anticipated profits are genuine, disregarding any evident cautionary indications.

If you've already invested in a scam, in your desperation you may wish that the fraudsters will have a change of mind, refund you or even deliver on their promises. Regrettably, when it comes to instances of financial fraud, having hopeful thoughts can lead to a major letdown since fraudsters seldom experience a change of heart, and the resulting losses are frequently irreversible. Relying on intuition becomes challenging when one lacks the necessary experience to support it.

WHEN A PROMPT DECISION IS REQUIRED

When you need to make a quick judgment, the vast store of knowledge already stored in your brain may come in handy.

Most of the time, it's helpful to gather as much information as possible so that you can make a knowledgeable decision. However, there are circumstances in which you may not have much time to think things out. Let's say you're in the process of scouting out a new place to call home. The neighborhood looks fine, the building is quiet and the unit itself is beautiful. You like it, but you'd prefer to devote more time to learning about any potential cons before making a decision.

At the end of the tour, the landlord will say politely, "You have the option to take it if you're interested, but I must inform you that three other people are also interested. As a result, I can only give you around 15 minutes to make your choice."

You'll start to think about whether or not you should take it, and your intuition may tell you, "Absolutely!" If it feels like the right place for you, feel free to listen. If this is your first time choosing a place to live, however, you may want to wait until you have more experience, do more research or ask for advice from someone who's versed in renting or buying property.

WHEN THERE IS AN ABSENCE OF INFORMATION

While it is true that relying solely on intuition cannot substitute for concrete evidence, there may be instances where factual information is not readily available for consideration. Or maybe you have some information, but not enough to lead you to a conclusion.

Maybe you find yourself in a situation where you have to make a decision between two job offers that appear to be quite similar in terms of qualifications, or you're contemplating whether or not to go on a second date with someone who doesn't exactly excite you.

Rely on your emotions when making these types of decisions, as your feelings can clarify the right step to take. Make the decision that resonates most strongly with your personal identity.

WHEN ATTEMPTING TO CONNECT WITH YOUR PERSONAL REQUIREMENTS

An intuitive understanding of your needs often surpasses the limitations of logic and reason. In the end, no one understands you better than you do. For instance, you may have a birthday dinner to go to, but you lack the desire to actually go. Perhaps you are fatigued, and a boisterous, packed room is the last place you want to spend your night. Some part of you knows that you might feel better once you get there, but that thought is countered by a stronger one that says, *"No way."* Listen to the voice and skip the party. Paying attention to your body's signals can assist you in making choices that cater to your immediate needs.

Chapter 4 Summary

In this chapter, we explored the cunning strategies used by scammers to uphold the façade of a genuine investment opportunity. As I reflected on the numerous deceptive strategies and manipulative ploys that I encountered – such as intricately designed online platforms, falsified endorsements, convoluted terminology and deceptive communications – we developed a deeper comprehension of the diverse disguises employed by fraudsters to prevent us from detecting warning signs. We gained knowledge about the tactics employed by scammers to maintain an appearance of authenticity. It is crucial to acknowledge the significance of these initial indicators, the emotional consequences of deception and trusting your intuition. The chapter finished with techniques for managing difficult situations, reporting fraudulent activities and restoring one's economic stability, showcasing the strength and determination exhibited by individuals affected by scams.

5

SIX MONTHS OF FALSE HOPE

The greatest glory in living lies not in never falling, but in rising every time we fall.

–Nelson Mandela

In this chapter, I'll take you back to that vulnerable moment when I first realized that my world was built on shaky ground. The feelings of disbelief, betrayal and uncertainty that washed over me were as accurate as they were disorienting. It was a time when I questioned the intentions of others and my judgment, leaving me on the precipice of an emotional freefall.

On that fateful day in January 2022, my world crumbled when I received an email stating that all the money had vanished from my digital wallet. I felt physically ill and emotionally numb, as I had lost everything. After the initial shock began to subside, I was trembling and crying uncontrollably. The unmistakable red flags, which I was aware of, now haunted me incessantly. A profound sense of sorrow and shame enveloped me. I wondered, *What possessed me to make such an incredibly stupid decision? How could I ever find the words to confess my actions to those I hold dear?*

I was too confused and embarrassed to say to anybody, "Every day I've cried," or "I'm at a loss for what to do." I have been coping with the psychological effects ever since I discovered

I had been duped. Not only are frauds widely thought to be grossly underreported, but victims' suffering goes far beyond drained bank accounts.

I felt like a glass figurine, at first delicate, then quickly shattered by the weight of deceit. My emotional state resembled a Jenga tower teetering on the edge of collapse, each new revelation pulling out a crucial piece. Little did I know I was about to embark on the next part of the deception that would test my resilience in the face of a web of lies and deceit.

When I communicated with the fraudsters, they offered reassurance that everything was under control. They claimed they would retrieve the money, and if necessary, they would liquidate their assets to reimburse all the funds lost in the wallets. They urged me not to fret, assuring me that all my money remained secure and that things would return to normal soon. I desperately wanted to believe them, and so I did. The alternative was admitting I had lost everything, which felt like an unbearable burden. Therefore, I continued with the charade and kept the truth hidden from everyone. Indeed, I thought everything would turn out fine.

I clung to this belief for six long months, repeatedly telling myself everything would be all right and my money would be returned. Maintaining this facade with the fraudsters and my family was utterly draining. I was left emotionally and physically shattered. I communicated with the fraudsters several times a week, seeking to alleviate my stress and anxiety in the desperate hope that my money was safe. Over these six months, my fraudsters continued to exude charm and confidence, occasionally offering gifts to keep me placated. Their mastery of manipulation allowed them to keep me relatively calm during our conversations. However, if I were to be brutally honest, my hope was steadily dwindling as the months passed.

Reality finally came crashing down on me in mid-June 2022, when the fraudsters abruptly severed all communication. My emails bounced back, their phone lines were disconnected, and their offices were deserted. It was the moment when the harsh truth hit home: All my money was gone. Once again, I was physically ill, experiencing panic attacks, struggling to catch my breath and feeling suffocated by the weight of the situation. *What am I going to do now?* After a few days of intense stress, I summoned the courage to confide in my husband, who offered unwavering support despite undergoing medical treatments at the time. He assured me we would endure and emerge even stronger, though I didn't feel strong. We then shared the news with our children and close friends, and finally, I mustered the courage to contact the police.

I felt incredibly foolish and embarrassed when I spoke to the police. I couldn't help but wonder what they must have thought of me. However, they were remarkably kind and reassured me that falling victim to such schemes could happen to anyone, emphasizing that it was not my fault. After a few days, I was connected with an officer who was already working on another case involving the same individuals, and he would be handling my case moving forward. He also introduced me to support groups dedicated to helping fraud victims, an invaluable source of comfort and guidance as I navigated the loss. The experience was akin to grieving a loved one: denial, anger, bargaining, depression and acceptance. I went through all these stages, but acceptance was the most challenging of all.

Recounting the details of the fraud to the police, as they meticulously documented every aspect, felt like reliving the ordeal again. Overwhelmed by my own perceived foolishness, I sobbed a lot. The police, however, were incredibly supportive throughout the process, consistently encouraging me to stay strong and assuring me that justice would ultimately prevail. At the time, I certainly didn't feel strong and harbored doubts about ever getting justice.

As 2022 drew to a close, I slowly regained some strength and a sense of normalcy. I could put into practice the self-development techniques I had acquired over the years, including meditation, mindfulness, exercise and yoga.

Falling victim to fraud can indeed be a shocking and disheartening experience, even for the most knowledgeable and dependable individuals. Fraudsters can be incredibly crafty, and their tactics can deceive even the most discerning people. It's essential to remember that you're not alone in facing such challenges, as fraud can happen to anyone. The key is to take steps to recover and protect yourself from further harm.

My choice to report the crime to the authorities marked a significant stride toward seeking justice and potentially preventing future fraud. Once I had come to terms with the deception, I could begin healing and taking action to bring the perpetrators to justice. Embracing this harsh reality was emotionally taxing but it represented the vital initial phase of this journey.

Reporting the crime demonstrated my determination to hold the fraudsters accountable for their actions. I felt a profound moral responsibility to ensure these individuals faced legal consequences for their fraudulent activities. Through this action, I aspired to safeguard others from falling victim to the same fraud. While the prospects of recovering my lost funds remained and still remain slim, law enforcement managed to trace and freeze some assets that were not directly linked to the fraud.

Reporting the crime entailed providing crucial details and evidence of the fraud, including documents, websites, contact information and bank account details. A formal report was filed, initiating the legal proceedings. As the investigation unfolded, it became part of a much broader inquiry encompassing numerous companies and individuals spanning several years. I actively cooperated with the authorities by providing witness statements and evidence. Additionally, I took the initiative to file complaints with my bank, which had never conducted an investigation or questioned the numerous deposits made into the fraudsters' bank accounts. This was perplexing, especially considering the fraudsters were on a "suspicious" list available to the bank at the time that I was making payments.

Seeking justice can be a demanding and intricate undertaking, often marred by numerous obstacles and hurdles. Among the challenges we encountered was the international nature of my case, which resulted in delays in the pursuit of justice. Additionally, the legal proceedings faced setbacks due to a shortage of human resources within the system.

The sheer volume of evidence posed a substantial challenge, impeding progress as legal teams and law enforcement grappled with limited resources and time constraints. As we prepare for the court proceedings at the time of writing this book, we've been advised that it will require considerable time to bring the perpetrators to justice. After all, patience is a virtue, as the old adage says.

Ultimately, the journey to secure justice in cases of financial fraud can be strenuous, and the outcome may vary based on the unique circumstances and available resources. It remains crucial for victims to maintain their resilience, seek support from advocacy groups and support networks, and continue to cooperate with law enforcement to the best of their ability.

In the next chapter, my story finally moves from fragility to strength, navigating the treacherous landscape of lies and ultimately finding the inner fortitude to rebuild my sense of trust and security.

While fraud may have caused you harm, it does not have the power to shape the person you are. Your true character emerges as you heal and move forward.

The Different Types of Scams

In the United States, fraudulent activities and cybercrimes constitute a significant portion of the country's overall criminal activity. Scams don't just impact individuals; many businesses also fall victim to the deceptive tactics employed by fraudsters.

Small businesses, in particular, are frequently the targets for scammers. That's because smaller enterprises and newly established ventures usually lack the necessary cybersecurity assistance and well-established accounting procedures that larger corporations possess. As a consequence, they are considerably more susceptible to fraudsters and thus provide ideal prey. The following are some of the most common scams that target small businesses:

SENDING COUNTERFEIT BILLS AND UNSOLICITED PRODUCTS

Fraudsters often fabricate invoices that bear a striking resemblance to legitimate orders or services requested from a small business. That way, the individual responsible for settling the company's financial obligations will perceive the invoices as authentic and proceed with the payment. However, it's all phony.

Alternatively, the scammer might make a fraudulent phone call, asserting their intention to "validate" a pre-existing purchase, "authenticate" a location or provide a "complimentary" brochure or specimen. If you happen to agree with any of these options, unrequested goods will be delivered to your place of business, accompanied by seemingly non-stop requests for payment. Avoid making any payments. It's crucial to keep in mind that if you receive unsolicited merchandise, you have a legal right to keep it and use it for free.

PROMISING PROMOTION FOR A BUSINESS IN A CHARITABLE PUBLICATION – THAT ISN'T ACTUALLY WHAT IT SEEMS

In this fraudulent scheme, an unscrupulous publisher approaches a company with an enticing proposal to advertise in a publication tied to a noble purpose. For example, their printed materials might include brochures, annual publications, personal organizers, schedules or periodicals that seem to serve nonprofit organizations, crime-reduction initiatives, substance abuse education, healthcare facilities or first responders. On occasion, publishers may engage in deceptive practices by falsely asserting affiliations with these various entities. In some instances, they may even manipulate these organizations into unwittingly aligning themselves with their cause. There is little to no assurance that the readership will be local or relevant to the small business who has agreed to advertise, and if the publication is produced at all, it may only be in tiny print runs or with restricted distribution. If a charitable contribution is made, it often represents a very small percentage of total earnings.

SETTING UP FAKE BUSINESS-MENTORING PROGRAMS

Scammers sometimes use fake endorsements, videos, conference slides and telemarketer calls to sell fake business-coaching programs. Their deceptive tactics involve making grandiose claims about the extraordinary outcomes one can achieve by purchasing their exclusive and supposedly foolproof business-success program. In addition, they might entice you with affordable introductory prices, only to demand exorbitant sums of money at a later stage. In actuality, the fraudsters abandon aspiring business owners, leaving them devoid of the assistance they initially sought and burdened with substantial financial liabilities.

PRETENDING THEY'RE AUTHORITY FIGURES OR PART OF RESPECTED ENTERPRISES

Scammers frequently masquerade as familiar or trustworthy individuals to bolster their credibility and manipulate you to make hasty choices. For example:

- Fraudsters might pretend to be representatives from a utility company and claim that your gas, electricity or water supply will be cut off due to a (non-existent) overdue payment.

- Con artists might pretend to be government officials and use intimidation tactics to threaten you with the suspension of your business licenses, impose fines or take legal action against you. They may say that you have unpaid taxes or require a license or registration renewal, which won't be true.
- Some may attempt to deceive you into purchasing workplace compliance posters that are actually available for free from the U.S. Department of Labor.
- Certain scammers deceive unsuspecting individuals by charging them for applications for purported government business grants, which ultimately prove to be fraudulent.
- Con artists pretend to be the U.S. Patent and Trademark Office and use intimidation tactics to make you believe that you must pay a fee right away or risk losing your trademark. Sometimes, they deceive and claim that you have a debt for extra registration services.
- There are individuals who pretend to be representatives of a tech company and make false claims that your business will lose its website URL unless you make an immediate payment.

LISTING A BUSINESS IN A DIRECTORY

Another popular method of trickery is soliciting a business's contact information to include in a seemingly traditional directory. So, be vigilant when a representative from a business directory sends you what appears to be authentic paperwork, urging you to confirm or divulge your website, email and other contact details. These inquiries may seem like harmless invitations for free inclusion, but with further scrutiny, you might have a surprising revelation – you could find yourself facing exorbitant charges of hundreds of dollars for a seemingly insignificant submission to a directory. Listing your business in directories can often be ineffective anyway.

It's important to consider whether potential customers would actually rely on these directories instead of popular search engines when searching for your company.

PROVIDING FREE REGULATORY SERVICES – AT A COST

Lots of businesses find it overwhelming to navigate the various regulatory obligations that they must follow to continue their operations. They often find themselves in need of licenses and authorizations, or they may be required to submit various reports and returns to governmental entities. The most cost-effective and typically convenient approach to fulfilling these criteria is to directly engage with the relevant organizations. In numerous instances, there is absolutely no fee associated with the act of informing, enrolling or providing data in compliance with a regulatory obligation.

Nevertheless, there exists a multitude of deceitful individuals who not only provide a fee-based service to carry out such tasks on behalf of businesses, but also deceive these businesses by creating an illusion of legitimacy. On occasion, these fraudsters may compose professional letters addressed to companies, citing relevant laws and consequences, while requesting both information and payment. Occasionally, they establish online platforms that companies may accidentally come across while searching for the appropriate, authorized website to fulfill their responsibilities, but they have no authority to provide such a service.

RENTING OUT NON-EXISTENT PRODUCTS OR SERVICES

Frequently, a "sales representative" pays a personal visit to the business being targeted. They convince the business to sign a contract, typically for a package deal of products and services. This contract includes leasing costly equipment, which may include telecommunication devices, computers, copiers, or other types of business or industrial equipment. The services on offer may involve using or taking care of the equipment.

The initial offering and prices may seem appealing, but the person is deceived about the true level of their obligation. Many times, people find themselves locked into lengthy lease agreements, typically lasting five to seven years. These agreements can be quite costly to terminate, and the equipment provided may not be worth the investment. Service and maintenance agreements often experience price increases without reason, or they may abruptly end if the supplier decides to switch to a different fraudulent scheme, thus leaving the purchaser to fix the products on their own dime after paying the fraudster upfront for this service.

POSING AS TECH SUPPORT

The first sign of a tech-support scam is a call or a pop-up message purporting to be from a reputable organization, warning you that your computer is in danger. Their objective is to acquire your funds or gain entry to your computer – and sometimes, they want to do both. Some individuals might request payment from you to resolve an issue that doesn't actually exist or persuade you to join a computer-maintenance program that is either non-existent or ineffective. It is possible for them to obtain confidential information, such as passwords, customer data or credit card details, once they have access to your computer.

RECEIVING UNWANTED ITEMS

Occasionally, companies may receive unexpected packages from criminals. These cunning individuals patiently wait for the opportune moment when the company either utilizes or gets rid of the items. Then, out of the blue, a surprise invoice materializes, requesting payment for unexpected merchandise, catching the business off guard. The quality of the products is frequently lacking, and the prices are typically higher than what is considered standard in the industry. The fraudulent plan often includes the unauthorized use of different items from the company's stock, such as inexpensive but necessary items like cleaning products, office materials, receipt rolls and generic printer ink. In certain versions of this deceitful scheme, the merchant initiates a transaction and later, after a few months, claims an error, asserting that additional items need to be dispatched. The business, without suspecting anything, willingly accepts the proposal for the remaining goods and is also provided with additional vouchers or alternative compensation options to resolve the claimed error. Upon arrival of the goods, the company discovers an unexpected absence of an invoice. However, this doesn't discourage them, and they promptly begin utilizing the items. After a brief period, the recipient is sent an invoice requesting a significant sum of money. Despite their objections, they are obligated to proceed with the payment.

PROMISING TO ALTER CUSTOMER FEEDBACK

Scammers might make enticing claims about enhancing your product's standing on a review platform by eliminating negative feedback, introducing positive reviews or employing a blend of both strategies. It is strictly prohibited to publish fraudulent reviews as per the regulations outlined by the FTC; it is crucial for endorsements, including reviews, to authentically reflect the opinions and individual encounters of the individual endorsing the product or service (Federal Trade Commission, 2009).

ASKING YOU TO CASH A (COUNTERFEIT) CHECK

Some scammers may provide you with a believable reason to make a payment to you through a check for more than the product or service they're buying. Afterward, they will request that you return the additional funds to either them or another individual. However, the check will be counterfeit, even if it appears as "cleared" in your account. Once the bank realizes that the check is invalid, the scammer will have already received the funds you transferred to them, and you will find yourself obligated to repay the financial institution.

Scammers sometimes use other dubious methods, such as pretending to provide high-paying gig-economy employment, but then falling short on paying the incomes they guaranteed. Or, they may attempt to up-sell you on things you don't need by telling you that your company's credit score would increase if you paid them. Also, when a natural disaster strikes, unlicensed tradesmen and con artists may promise rapid repairs, clean-up and debris removal that they cannot deliver on.

CHARGING FAULTY ADVANCE FEES

Advance-fee fraud comes in many forms, but the basic idea is always the same: The scammer, pretending to be someone important, such as a government official, lawyer, or businessperson, tricks people into helping them. In exchange, they promise the victim a huge amount of money, sometimes in the hundreds of thousands or even millions of dollars. In the beginning, they won't ask for any money. But later on, they'll start adding small charges like "taxes" or "legal fees." These payments will keep increasing until the person realizes it's a scam or runs out of money. These scams, like investment scams, target unsuspecting individuals, as the fraudsters know that company owners will likely fall for their schemes because they make it seem like they have easy access to large sums of money.

Mastering the Art of Identifying and Steering Clear of Phishing Scams

Phishing is a type of scam that involves tricking folks into sharing personal information or downloading harmful software through social manipulation.

Fraudsters will send you emails or text messages in an attempt to pilfer your passwords, account numbers or Social Security numbers. If someone obtains that data, they may gain entry to your email, banking or other online accounts. Alternatively, they may choose to distribute your personal data to other individuals involved in fraudulent activities. Every day, scammers carry out numerous phishing attacks similar to these, and unfortunately, they usually achieve their goals. Scammers tend to stay abreast of current events and fashions, and often modify their strategies; nonetheless, the following are some typical approaches.

To deceive their targets into interacting with a link or accessing a file, scammers frequently employ captivating storylines within phishing emails and text messages. It's crucial to stay vigilant and remain wary of any dubious emails or messages that appear to be from reputable entities such as prominent credit card companies, utility providers, or financial institutions. It could have arrived through a digital payment platform or mobile application. The sender of the message might have malicious intentions, and they could:

- Claim to have detected unusual behavior or login attempts when, in reality, they haven't
- Assert that there is an issue – when there isn't – with your account or payment details
- Request that you provide confirmation of confidential or financial data – when you actually do not
- Attach a phony invoice that you are unsure about
- Request that you complete a transaction through a link that contains malicious software.
- Tell you that you qualify for a government reimbursement that doesn't exist
- Present you with a fake voucher for free merchandise

The primary objective of email scams is to deceive people by creating an illusion of authenticity in their messages. Despite an email appearing to be from a familiar company and displaying their logo in the header, there are clear indicators that it is a fraudulent attempt:

- The email begins with a standard salutation.
- According to the email, your account is currently suspended due to an issue with your billing.
- The email requests that you follow a link to provide updated payment information.

Legitimate organizations won't send you an email or text with a link to change your payment details, even if they may connect with you by email. Those who respond to phishing emails and provide criminals with their personal information may face serious repercussions, such as identity theft.

The spam filters in your email can help prevent a lot of phishing emails from reaching your inbox. However, those attempting to deceive spam filters are constantly seeking ways to outwit them, making additional safeguards crucial. Here are three effective methods to protect yourself against phishing attacks:

1. Use security software to safeguard your PC. To ensure that the program responds to any new security risks, set it to update automatically.
2. Similarly, make sure the software on your phone is updated automatically to protect it. You may have vital security protection against online attacks thanks to these upgrades.
3. Make use of multi-factor authentication to safeguard your accounts. As previously explained, this is when certain accounts provide an additional layer of protection by requiring the use of two or more login credentials.

First, find out whether you have an account with that firm, or confirm that you know who is contacting you if you get an email or text message asking you to click on a link or open an attachment. If you don't have an account or know the sender, it may be a phishing hoax. If you do, get in touch with the business using a legitimate phone number or website – not the details included in the email – to make sure the message is real. Links and attachments may download malicious software.

How to Check If an Email Is Legit

When attempting to ascertain the authenticity of an email, there are several factors to consider. Use these three methods to protect against password disclosure, employee W-2 form theft and illicit fund transfers.

1. **Confirm:** Verify the email address to protect yourself. Hover over the "from" display name to see the email address. Perpetrators often mimic screen names to seem credible. Different people sending messages can be identified by hovering over their screen names. Compare recent emails with previous messages from familiar senders. Is the display name consistent in all emails? Is the email signature the same? You can also call them directly. Use a contact number from your personal directory instead of relying on what's provided in a potentially dubious email.
2. **Examine:** Some fraudsters make it harder to uncover their crimes. You'll have to delve a bit deeper to uncover these. Start by reviewing the email in detail. One tactic manipulates email addresses to deceive people. This technique is called substitution or transposition. Email addresses can be altered by replacing "m" with "rn," "L" with "1," or ".com" with ".co." A small change in the email address will send the email to a different place and indicate that it may be fraudulent. Activate SPF (Sender Policy Framework) records in your email system. Review the email's internet header details to determine its destination.

These are great party tricks to impress your friends with tech skills!

3. **Seek out:** Search the email domain to verify the sender's authenticity. This approach is useful for messages from unfamiliar people. Confirm domain ownership and provide setup information. Platforms such as WHOis and ICANN provide domain name establishment dates and website owner information. If a website is new but the vendor claims to have been operating for 30 years, check if their statement is credible. Take advantage of popular search engines such as Google, Bing or Yahoo. Search engines detect and display scams in search results. When unsure about a message, check online for fraud alerts.

How to Protect Personal Information Online

In this digital age, it has become even easier for individuals with bad intentions to gather specific details about you through online platforms. Whether it's a piece of content you shared that provided them with a hint, or you accessed a platform and they managed to breach your devices, I have some suggestions that can help you prevent your personal information from falling into the hands of unauthorized individuals.

1. **Refrain from divulging excessive personal information on social media platforms.** Ensure that you review and adjust your privacy settings to stay informed about the individuals who have access to your posts. Additionally, exercise caution when sharing information such as your location, hometown, birthday or any other personal particulars.
2. **Verify the website's security status.** Before entering personal information on a website, check the searchbar area of your browser. A website is secure if it has a lock

symbol in that box, and "https" in the URL. A privacy policy, contact information or a secure verification mark might also indicate a website's credibility.

3. **Exercise caution when utilizing complimentary wireless internet access.** Many public Wi-Fi networks that are available for free lack sufficient security measures, making it possible for other users on the same network to potentially view your online activities without much difficulty.
4. **Develop robust passwords.** To thwart thieves, avoid easy-to-guess passwords like birthdays. Choose a combination of lowercase and uppercase letters, numbers and symbols, and change them often. Instead of using the same password across platforms, use a unique one for each account. Using a password manager can help you remember all your passwords.

The Significance of Notifying the Authorities of the Fraud and Pursuing Redress

In the United States, it is generally not a legal requirement for businesses to inform federal authorities regarding cases of fraud or cyber-attacks carried out by scammers. It is just strongly advised that you notify authorities about such incidents, and various law enforcement organizations have established mechanisms for individuals and companies to report cybercrimes. Nevertheless, numerous businesses that become victims of such occurrences frequently opt not to reveal the transgression.

There are numerous factors that contribute to companies making this decision, but one primary reason is their lack of perceived value in doing so. It is widely known that pinpointing threat actors, particularly in cases where attacks originate from foreign sources, is extremely challenging. Although it is possible that law enforcement may not assist in restoring operations or stopping the transfer of stolen data, it is important to note that the Federal Bureau of Investigation's (FBI) Recovery Asset Team (RAT) has a strong track record of successfully recovering assets. Nevertheless, the requirement is that prompt action be taken.

When a company experiences a data breach, its main concerns are to address the issue, improve any internal weaknesses, prevent future incidents, and meet legal requirements by informing affected individuals and regulatory bodies. Certainly, individuals might have the desire to apprehend the person responsible for this, but the offense has already been committed.

It can be difficult for a business owner to locate these mysterious cybercriminals. Having to find someone who is able to evade law enforcement only adds to the onerous nature of handling a data breach. Furthermore, it may be deemed a waste of time to disclose this information, given that there is no legal requirement to do so.

Reporting may also be neglected due to the difficulty in determining responsibility and the general absence of legal action. Not to mention that, rather than highly trained gangs planning massive operations, many cybercrime charges include holding juveniles accountable for smaller crimes.

Companies usually choose not to report an incident if the police deem it insignificant due to the small amount of money or information involved. They may also hesitate to report cybercrimes because of the potential costs and time involved, as well as the belief that it may not lead to any meaningful recovery for the company.

The main reason not to report a cybercrime would be that the situation does not warrant the involvement of law enforcement due to the time and cost involved, and it would be more effective to handle it internally. Plus, certain companies might be concerned that involving law enforcement could potentially cause additional disruptions to their business operations while they conduct investigations.

There is a common belief that the FBI or the Secret Service might intervene in these cases and attempt to assume control of the companies' investigations. Clearly, this is untrue. These investigative units have no intention of assuming control of an inquiry – they are just interested in identifying the culprit.

While it's understandable that businesses might be concerned about the potential effect of an investigation on their day-to-day operations, it's important to remember that police don't set up roadblocks or park patrol vehicles outside of cyberattack victims' offices.

REASONS WHY BUSINESSES SHOULD REPORT CYBERCRIME AND PURSUE JUSTICE

While reporting may not provide an immediate solution to a specific incident faced by a company, it can offer several benefits in the long run. Effective collaboration between law enforcement agencies and international partners is crucial in combating organized cybercrime groups. This collaboration can significantly reduce the frequency of attacks targeting your business.

Federal agencies such as the FBI have a wealth of resources and expertise in this field, making them highly valuable allies to have. Having these specialists readily available can greatly enhance a company's investigation process. The FBI can offer a diverse range of valuable assistance. They have the authority to mandate the disclosure of information by an internet service provider. They can also work together with colleagues from around the world.

Businesses that collaborate with law enforcement can provide valuable information to intelligence-sharing initiatives such as the FBI's InfraGard program. Given the prevalence of data breaches that affect multiple companies, each with its own unique collection of data, it is plausible that a specific company's data breach could provide valuable clues to aid law enforcement in investigating other similar incidents. For example, if a company discovers evidence of an ongoing business email compromise attack, it is advisable to inform the authorities to see if they can link it to other cybercrimes and therefore provide protections. Taking this action could help prevent the attack from causing significant harm.

Another benefit of informing the authorities is that it can help with the recovery process for insurance and compliance-related incidents. It is important and sometimes necessary to report cybercrimes to insurance companies. When processing claims related to incidents, insurers usually ask for a crime reference number. Some further underappreciated benefits include:

- **Maintaining your business's good name.** Instances of fraud that go unreported can have severe consequences for an organization's reputation, especially if it becomes evident that there has been an attempt to conceal the truth. Negative media attention can tarnish the image of publicly listed companies, leading to financial repercussions. This, in turn, can directly affect the organization's market capitalization. The presence of scams poses a significant risk to the survival of any organization or establishment, as it erodes the credibility and reliability that a company holds as a dependable collaborator.
- **Fostering a positive workplace environment.** One often overlooked consequence of fraud is the detrimental impact it can have on employee morale and the overall wellbeing of a company's internal dynamics. Undisclosed fraudulent activities indicate underlying issues within the corporate culture that extend beyond mere financial implications. Hence, it is imperative for companies and their executives to prioritize and demonstrate ethical behavior in the eyes of their employees, collaborators and stakeholders.

Choosing to ignore illicit activities can serve as a catalyst for the perpetuation of corruption. On the other hand, a strict strategy put in place by management that includes thorough internal investigations and a relentless pursuit of legal consequences makes a strong showing that this type of behavior won't be tolerated.

Furthermore, it is the responsibility of an organization's leadership to operate with a strong sense of ethics, which should be deeply embedded in the organization's culture and should *not* necessitate external regulations for enforcement. When executives decide to conceal acts of fraud rather than implement corrective actions, they are jeopardizing the integrity of their organization and exacerbating organizational risk instead of reducing it.

- **Completing a standard practice in the field of risk management.** As observed, deceit carries significant consequences for a business's finances and reputation. The act of overseeing and documenting misconduct is, therefore, an indispensable part of mitigating potential risks. Safeguarding a company against potential threats that would hinder its intended goals is a core responsibility of management and, notably, the oversight committee. Numerous companies achieve this objective by utilizing their corporate-audit and enterprise-risk departments. To make a platform for finding risks and reducing them, you need to set up a system that uses advanced analytics, fraud detection signals, risk assessments and patterns found in behavioral science. By incorporating internal audits into this process, organizations can effectively detect and address any deficiencies within their risk management framework.

Notifying the police about the scam helps people learn more about the complicated nature of dishonest activities. This could have a big effect on the rules and reporting systems, as well as make risk management methods better, which would be good for everyone involved. And in view of the rapid development of several forms of internet criminal activity, this assertion bears considerable merit.

Putting in place efficient, automated systems that can quickly find and fix initial data errors is very helpful for financial institutions. These methods are very helpful because they stop you from losing money, keep your customers happy, and prevent you from having to deal with big financial problems like losing money, getting fined or hurting your chances of growing your business in the future.

Chapter 5 Summary

In this chapter, I explored the impact of falling victim to a deceptive digital wallet scheme, leading to a rollercoaster of emotions and months of misplaced optimism. From the start of the year until mid-2022, I experienced a sense of unwarranted optimism, which gave way to me gradually acknowledging the fraud I faced, reporting of the wrongdoing and pursuing fairness. After the scammers "lost" my money, they assured me that they would get it back, and I naively believed, but by June 2022, after they abruptly cut all communication with me, I just had to accept that I had been defrauded. Once the harsh reality had set in, anxiety attacks and a profound sense of self-disgust quickly followed. The feeling of betrayal was too much, so I sought comfort from my husband. His encouragement motivated me to inform the authorities about the incident and start my recovery process.

Reporting fraud, working with law enforcement, and seeking help are emphasized in this chapter. We also studied legal obstacles in global cases and common fraudulent schemes that target businesses. This section stressed the need to recognize phishing scams, protect personal data and report cybercrimes. In summary, this chapter culminates in a shift from fragility to strength.

6

EMPOWERMENT AND RESILIENCE

Adversities possess a unique knack for unearthing latent talents that might have otherwise remained dormant amidst periods of triumph.

– Horace

I had to face the crushing loss of my lifetime savings. I thought, *The death of my mother and my spouse's terminal illness have both been heavy burdens for me to bear. Yet, I was able to do it, which surely speaks to my resilience, so I'll probably be able to overcome this as well. It just won't be easy.*

By January 2023, I had resolved not to let the past define me. I was determined to return to the place I had been before and start enjoying life once more. I knew it would require immense effort, but I was sure it would be worth it. I began reading books like Joe Dispenza's *Breaking the Habit of Being Yourself* and Tony Robbins' *Awaken the Giant Within*. I tuned into podcasts featuring leaders like Barack Obama, Michelle Obama and Oprah Winfrey. I practiced meditation with the guidance of Deepak Chopra and Eckhart Tolle. I re-engaged in my local yoga class and started socializing with friends again. I revamped my diet to reflect the healthier choices I used to make, cutting out the junk food that had been my solace in the months following the fraud. Gradually, I began to believe in myself again, which felt empowering. While there were still days when I felt down and unworthy, these instances were becoming less frequent, and better days were on the horizon.

My transition from a fraud victim to a fraud conqueror is a profound transformation that underscores resilience, unwavering determination and personal growth. In the aftermath of my traumatic experience, I embarked on a journey of self-discovery and empowerment. Recognizing the importance of understanding vulnerable moments and the lurking pitfalls, I made it my mission to master the art of vigilance.

I am eager to share the steps I took to regain my footing and become a vigilant guardian of my well being. This voyage represents a path to self- empowerment, a relentless pursuit of transforming the painful lessons learned into a wellspring of inner strength. Today, I find myself embracing a victorious mindset. I adamantly refuse to let the scam define me or dictate my future. Instead, I have emerged from the ordeal as a stronger, more resolute individual, ready to chart my course.

Handling anxiety, guilt and humiliation can be challenging, especially when you've experienced a traumatic event like falling victim to fraud. Here are my top nine tips I found invaluable in my healing journey:

1. **Seek professional help.** Consider contacting a therapist, counselor or mental health professional specializing in trauma and stress. They can provide the necessary tools and techniques to manage your emotions effectively.
2. **Talk to supportive friends and family.** Share your feelings with trusted friends and family members who can offer emotional support. Sometimes, just talking about your emotions can be incredibly therapeutic.
3. **Practice self-compassion.** Be kind and gentle with yourself. Understand that anyone can be vulnerable to scams, and blaming yourself will only intensify feelings of

guilt and humiliation. Extend kindness to yourself in the same way you would bestow it upon a companion facing a comparable circumstance.

4. **Educate yourself.** Learn about the psychology of fraud and how scammers operate. Understanding the tactics they use can help you realize that you were manipulated and that it was not your fault.
5. **Limit self-criticism.** Avoid negative self-talk and self-criticism. Remind yourself that you are not defined by this event. Mistakes are a part of life, but what truly counts is the ability to learn from them and develop.
6. **Engage in mindful living.** Embracing the art of mindfulness involves incorporating various practices like meditation and conscious breathing exercises. These techniques can effectively anchor you to the present, fostering a sense of calm and alleviating feelings of unease. They can also assist in managing feelings of humiliation.
7. **Engage in physical activity.** Regular exercise can help alleviate anxiety and stress by releasing endorphins, which are natural mood lifters.
8. **Prioritize self-care.** Give importance to your physical and emotional well-being. Make sure to prioritize sufficient rest, maintain a balanced diet and participate in enjoyable and calming pursuits.
9. **Welcome acceptance and forgiveness.** Over time, work toward accepting what has happened and forgiving yourself. Forgiveness doesn't mean condoning the scam but freeing yourself from its emotional burden. Be patient with yourself, and know that with time and support, you can overcome these difficult emotions and move forward. Understand that healing is a process.

The lies said to you may have hurt you, but they cannot define who you are. Your true character emerges as you heal and move forward.

How to Heal Emotionally

In the midst of my most trying times, I had a tremendous sense of inadequacy. I was overcome with feelings of hopelessness, despair and shame, but the dominant emotion for me was rage. I was overcome with rage, not only toward the people who had deceived me, but also toward my own naiveté in being taken advantage of for such an extended period. It was a raging wrath that seemed to consume me from the depths.

I was constantly irritated and lacked the desire to engage in conversation with anyone, including my partner. I had a strong desire to retreat from society and vanish, but thankfully, my loved ones kept me from going too far in my isolation. Even though they respected my need for privacy, they also went out of their way to offer words of support, knowing that mistakes happen all the time. They were even nice enough to gift me a collection of motivational books and letters to help me get back on my feet. The ones I read provoked a lot of thought and made me want to learn more about what had happened.

Slowly but surely, I began to reflect on my intense rage, and the more I thought about it, the more I realized that my anger not just me reacting to the deception that had happened. It was a cover-up for the emotions underneath to which I hadn't given enough attention – emotions related to my mother's death and my spouse's terminal illness.

It was a turning point in my road to healing when I finally accepted this fact. I made the conscious decision to pull myself out of my hole of misery and take charge of my life. I wasn't about to let the swindlers take my zest for life as well. After all, my mother instilled in me the importance of bravery and perseverance. So, I knew I had to press on despite the challenges that may arise, even if progress is made one small stride at a time.

I knew that in order to start healing, I had to face my feelings head-on, even if they made me feel bad, and figure out a way to make peace with them. The following are some creative techniques and methods that I used to deal with and control the difficult emotions that I was feeling:

- **Create a safe haven for yourself.** Locate a calm area where you can comfortably sit by yourself and reflect for approximately 5–10 minutes. Start playing calming music and then gently shut your eyes. After closing your eyes, envision yourself in a safe setting where you feel relaxed and completely at peace. Utilize your sensory perception to determine the current temperature within this secure environment of yours. Which hues are visible to you? How would you describe the scent? What sounds do you perceive? Open your eyes when you have a better idea of what this secure area looks like, and then sketch it.

  You don't even have to be a master artist for this. The sketch can even be a small scribble. The main idea is for you to comprehend the situation, so give it your best effort. After you're done, hang your painting somewhere you'll see it every day to serve as a constant reminder of this relaxed sensation. This will enable you to feel secure enough to explore the more uncomfortable feelings that you would prefer to keep to yourself.
- **Visualize a reassuring picture.** When you're experiencing intense distress, try envisioning something that gives you a sense of safety and care. This may manifest as an imaginary entity, a real location, or a person or being you know. While contemplating this restorative visualization, pay attention to your five senses. Take note of the various colors, shapes, noises and fragrances. Immerse yourself completely in the picture, and let it nourish your soul.
- **Tear paper into pieces.** This one may sound a little strange, but it is surprisingly effective. Select colored sheets of construction paper that correspond with your feelings. Take a few minutes to tear these sheets of paper into small

pieces. Feel free to go at your own pace, whether that be fast or slow. Picture a scenario where your emotions guide your actions as you tear something apart.

- **Doodle.** Take advantage of vivid colors like crimson to doodle on a sheet of paper for 10 minutes. Alternatively, you can paint on a larger piece of paper. Go ahead and draw bold markings on the paper by applying as much pressure as you can. Envision the emotions overflowing from your arms onto the page.
- **Engage in a symbolic letting-go exercise.** Trimming paper into strips can be quite beneficial. Write down a single concern on each piece of paper. Place the strips inside a container. Give the jar a good shake, and then let go of the paper strips in a meaningful manner. For example, you have the option to bury them in your garden, burn them in a small fire or toss them into the sea.
- **Make a playlist that reflects your emotions.** I composed a personal soundtrack to help me cope with the passing of my mother and the unfortunate deception I experienced. The soundtrack you create should be a collection of songs that represent the feelings you want to explore, like frustration, sorrow or melancholy. When you're coping with the absence of a person or a relationship, songs can serve as reminders of the memories shared with that individual. Alternatively, when you're experiencing anger, you may consider listening to music that conveys your emotions and longing to regain your inner power. For example, you might listen to "Lose Yourself" by Eminem or "Stronger" by Kanye West. An emotional tune about loss and longing, such as "Hurt" by Johnny Cash, can provide an outlet for processing the financial setbacks you have faced. Songs that inspire introspection, optimism and personal development, such as "Someone Like You" by Adele or "Hey Jude" by The Beatles. Take a moment to play your completed soundtrack and allow yourself to fully immerse yourself in the emotions that surface.

- **Craft an enchanted sphere.** This activity draws inspiration from dreamcatchers, which come from Native American and First Nations cultures. To make one, a small circular object is adorned with feathers and beads and hung over a bed to stop nightmares while allowing positive dreams to pass. For your enchanted sphere, you'll just need a pen, paper and some yarn. Create the hoop by sketching a circular shape. Within your personal sphere, compile a comprehensive inventory of the factors that elicit unfavorable feelings or currently weigh heavily on your mind. Afterward, adhere strands of yarn to your circular shape, creating a design that resembles a spider's web. This will capture your unfavorable feelings. Then, compile a list of the various sources of your strength and resilience. These may include your positive attributes, individuals you appreciate, activities that bring you happiness, and the people who hold a special place in your heart.
- **Make a collage showcasing your emotions.** Browse through various magazines to find pictures that convey your feelings. Attach these pictures to a sheet of paper using glue or tape. After finishing your collage, take some time to reflect and write about the visuals you have assembled. Pause momentarily and consider the following: "What is the intended message that you wish to impart to me?" Visual images and symbols are often more effective than words in conveying our profound emotions. For example, imagine you come across a picture of daisies that grabs your attention, so you include it in your collage, even though you're unsure of the reason behind your choice. After observing your collage for an extended period, you remember that daisies held a special place in your mother's heart. It is possible to realize that your current feelings of sadness are connected to past sorrows and losses that you were not fully aware of before. It is crucial to acknowledge and deal with your feelings. If you find it challenging to

handle overwhelming emotions, I recommend seeking support from a therapist who incorporates art into their therapy sessions. This method allows you to creatively and securely express and delve into your emotions.

Getting Your Confidence Back

If you've ever fallen for a scam, you know how devastating it can be to your sense of self. Take, for example, the case of my friend Rebecca. In May of last year, Rebecca, a resident of Taiwan, was immediately enamored with a German-born man she met on Tinder. He came off as interesting, insightful and a good listener (all of which she greatly appreciated). Within a mere six months, they made the choice to move in together, and shortly thereafter, he proposed, which she joyfully accepted.

Shortly thereafter, he approached Rebecca, a successful businesswoman, and asked to borrow $70,000 so that he could return to Germany and purchase a family home for the two of them and their future family. She took out a $30,000 loan from her parents, and promised to pay the remaining $40,000 when she moved. But once he left Taiwan, her fiancé cut off all communication with her and barred her from his accounts. At that moment, she realized that she had fallen victim to a romance scam.

To this day, Rebecca continues to encounter challenges in reestablishing the confidence she once had. For a very long time, she had trouble falling asleep and generally felt down. Her capacity to remember things was impacted, leading to numerous errors in her job performance. As someone who has experienced poor self-esteem, social isolation and feelings of powerlessness after being the victim of a scam, I can attest to the fact that these are some common psychological outcomes.

In my case, after I realized that I had fallen victim to a scam and lost my mother's inheritance, a wave of self-doubt and insecurity washed over me. It was not just the financial loss that upset me, but the overwhelming feeling of foolishness and vulnerability that came with it. I started doubting my own ability to make good judgments and decisions, and I would frequently criticize myself.

My self-esteem had fallen so low that I was finding it difficult to even look at myself in the mirror. I no longer recognized the person I used to be, so I decided to avoid looking at myself in the mirror for a while. Regaining my confidence turned out to be an enormous task that called for both a mental adjustment and a dedication to self-compassion. The following are some effective strategies for restoring self-confidence after being scammed:

- **Recognize your strengths and areas of expertise.** Developing a strong sense of self- assurance can be greatly enhanced by focusing on your unique abilities and past encounters, particularly during challenging periods in your journey. To prevent falling into the trap of comparison, make a list of your unique attributes and strengths. By acknowledging and celebrating your positive qualities, you can embrace your individuality and foster self-appreciation. One way to accomplish this task is by physically writing down all the aspects that bring you a sense of satisfaction. Similar to identifying positive aspects about yourself or receiving feedback from others, it is important to acknowledge your strengths and skills. These may pertain to different facets of your life, such as personal, professional or social skills. Additionally, this practice can help you to cultivate your own approach, recognising areas for personal growth and engage in activities that align with your natural talents.
- **Reflect on your life's accomplishments.** Whether you've taken significant strides in your professional journey,

academic pursuits, personal endeavors or even your hobbies and passions, reflecting on these achievements serves as a reminder that you have the ability to successfully accomplish so many tasks.

- **Establish attainable objectives.** This is a crucial component in gradually rebuilding self-assurance following a period of hardship. Having goals gives you a well-defined route to reclaiming a sense of autonomy, and exhibits development and advancement. Begin by determining the desired outcomes or changes you wish to make in your life. Next, divide your overarching objectives into more bite-sized and attainable actions. By breaking them down into smaller tasks, they become less intimidating and allow for gradual growth in self-assurance. Additionally, it is beneficial to make a habit of writing them down and displaying them in a prominent location to serve as a constant reminder of your objectives.
- **Engage in constructive self-conversation.** Positive self-talk is when you use encouraging and uplifting language in your internal dialogue. On the other hand, negative self-talk means you're utilizing critical and accusatory language when speaking to yourself. Pause for a moment and consider your internal monologue: Do you find yourself being self-critical? Do you possess a sense of self-support? Are phrases such as "I am trying my hardest" or "It's possible that others don't think I'm smart" part of your inner dialogue? People who use positive self-talk have a better chance of building confidence and self-worth, feeling more in control of their lives and reaching their goals. To begin, initiate the process by developing an understanding of your internal dialogue. When one finds themselves engaging in negative self-talk, it is important to question and challenge such thoughts.
- **Envision achievement.** The human mind has immense capabilities. When one engages in the act of visualization,

they can generate mental images that can be utilized to their benefit. One can utilize it to imagine a future wherein their assurance is restored, and their self-confidence is fortified. Mental imagery can significantly influence one's behavior and mindset. For optimal results, start by locating a serene and cozy environment that minimizes potential disturbances. Next, assume a relaxed posture, such as reclining on your bed or settling into a seat of your choice. Then, shut your eyes if you feel comfortable doing so, and begin envisioning the future you desire. Take your time with this process and fully immerse yourself in the experience by utilizing all your senses. By implementing this strategy, you will enhance your ability to concentrate on attaining your goal.

Chapter 6 Summary

In this chapter, I recounted my transformation from someone who faced adversity to someone who emerged victorious following a challenging experience. In January 2023, I made the decision to stop feeling sorry for myself. I made a conscious decision not to let my past shape me, so I embarked on a journey of personal development and transformation. I immersed myself in a wide range of self-improvement literature and audio content, embraced the practice of mindfulness and physical exercises like yoga, and adopted overall healthier habits. With time, I began to uncover a new version of myself and reclaim my confidence. The chapter highlighted the importance of resilience, individual development and self- empowerment, and demonstrated the transition from susceptibility to attentiveness in safeguarding one's welfare. I also provided advice on recovering from deception, controlling emotions and regaining confidence based on my own experiences, as well as the experiences of others who have gone through comparable struggles. Through sharing my story, my sincere desire is for others who read it to adopt an attitude of resilience in the face of hardship and to find strength within themselves by overcoming difficult events.

7

FIGHTING FOR A BETTER WORLD AND FUTURE

Once you emerge from the tempest, you will not be the identical individual who entered. That is the essence of the storm.

–Haruki Murakami

As I got wiser post-fraud, I realized three key things:

- Lost money can be found.
- Acquiring the skill of self-improvement and adapting is an amazing ability.
- The best teacher is your last mistake.

Over the past few months, I've begun to experience a sense of completeness again. There are still moments when feelings of horror and shame resurface, but they occur less frequently these days. Instead, I'm moving forward and becoming a better person than I was before the fraud. I feel empowered, strong, focused and genuinely excited about the future. Of course, there are ongoing challenges, including my husband's continued treatment and the usual family and life issues, but I feel better equipped to tackle them positively.

I am determined to emerge from this traumatic experience with something meaningful for myself, my family and the broader public. I want to ensure that more people understand the risks of making decisions in highly emotionally charged situations, and the value of making choices when calm and balanced. I aim to convey to people that if they find themselves in the unfortunate position of being a fraud victim, they can survive and thrive.

It deeply saddens me to hear about others going through the same ordeal I've endured. In today's technologically advanced world, we should be better equipped and protected against fraudsters. Because of the intense hurt and shame that victims go through, this has truly become my passion. Fraud prevention should not be an afterthought but should be at the forefront of everyone's awareness. Banks should have robust protective mechanisms to prompt people to pause and consider where they are sending their money. While there has been some progress in this area, it's still insufficient. In 2020, none of my transactions from my bank were ever questioned, despite my unusual activity and my fraudsters being on a "suspicious" list. Today, I'm asked a few questions when making a transaction, but it's clear that we need to take this to the next level to protect consumers better.

Today, I have turned my experience with fraud into a catalyst for positive change. I desire to advocate for a better world and future without, at the very least, a reduced number of frauds. Here are five ways I am fighting for a better world:

1. **Raising awareness** by sharing my story and knowledge about fraud to educate others. Recognizing the importance of being informed is the initial stage in avoiding potential issues.
2. **Supporting victims** by offering guidance. My experience can provide valuable insights and empathy to those facing similar challenges.

3. **Mentoring victims** to help them navigate the complexities of fraud and mental health.
4. **Participating in research** that aims to understand fraudsters' psychology and tactics better, helping to develop more effective prevention strategies.
5. **Support consumer protection.** Remember that even small actions can significantly impact the fight against fraud and create a more secure and ethical financial landscape.

In the last six months, I have been sharing information about fraud prevention to my friends, family and peers. This is a vital undertaking that has allowed me to establish a network of well-informed individuals who, ideally, will pass on this knowledge to others, ultimately preventing future fraud. For those who have been victims, I hope that sharing my experience will assist them in navigating this intricate situation and finding a faster path to healing.

I am deeply committed to sharing my experience and recommendations with readers so that they can educate their social circles. The most critical aspect is that individuals should not feel isolated when dealing with fraud, both during and after the experience. This ordeal can profoundly alter someone's perspective on people and the world, and I hope that, after reading this book, individuals will possess the skills to navigate – or avoid altogether – the treacherous terrain of a fraudster's world.

I am pursuing many avenues of advocacy as a victim of fraud. Here are four examples of my bold actions:

- **Collaborating with authorities** to improve fraud prevention measures and support for victims.
- **Publicly sharing my story** and knowledge at public events, conferences and in the media to raise awareness about fraud prevention.
- **Writing and publishing** articles, books and blog posts on fraud prevention and victim support.

- **Building a community** of like-minded individuals dedicated to preventing fraud and supporting victims.

These actions demonstrate my commitment to preventing fraud and supporting those affected by it, turning a negative experience into a positive force for change.

> *The scars of fraud serve as a reminder of your strength and the wisdom gained from adversity.*

Keeping Your Money Safe

My passion for warning people of the dangers of potential fraud is not just because I lost a lot of money. While that is without a doubt part of the reason, my true motivation is to save someone else from having to go through that same turmoil. Not everyone who falls victim to a scam has the luxury of having a strong, loving and understanding support system. That is why, despite many problems, I still consider myself somewhat lucky. Not every fraud victim has a sweet and attentive husband who will constantly reassure them and remind them of their strength.

I have seen a lot of scam victims made fun of and ridiculed for having "been so stupid to fall for it." In reality, I know that this can happen to anybody who finds themselves in a vulnerable place. Heck, plenty of fraud victims feel like they can never recover from their financial losses and end up dying by suicide. This is especially true if their support system is not strong enough or nonexistent. It happens more often than anyone is willing to admit and it's truly a shame. I get it because I too contemplated suicide. I believe that if I'd had someone to tell me, based on their own experience, that a year from the fraud, I would have the attitude of a winner, it would have made life much more bearable.

Prevention is better than the cure, and the best way to prevent yourself from being scammed is to become more educated on the matter. With that being said, here are some things to be cognizant of to better equip yourself in the face of fraud:

- **Exercise caution when receiving unexpected messages.** It is important to be careful with unexpected emails, messages or calls, particularly if they ask for personal or financial details. Fraudsters rely on our lack of knowledge and tendency to trust things that appear authoritative. Keep in mind that reputable companies will not unexpectedly ask for personal information such as your Social Security number, password or bank details. Rely on your gut feelings and avoid sharing any details until you've confirmed the messenger's validity.
- **Employ reliable methods of communication.** Unlike unsecured methods, encrypted communication channels protect user information while it is being transmitted. Platforms that lack security measures can put sensitive information at risk of being intercepted by malicious individuals, which can result in unauthorized access and misuse. Protected communication channels also hinder unauthorized listening by external entities. Select communication platforms that have a well-established reputation for ensuring security and privacy, like Signal, WhatsApp and Telegram, among others. ProtonMail and Tutanota are two popular email services that prioritize security and encryption for safe communication. End-to-end encryption is crucial for ensuring the security of a platform, as it ensures that only the intended recipient can decrypt and access the communication's content.
- **Seek multiple opinions before making a decision.** When it comes to investment scams, scammers prefer to isolate the victim by making them keep the investment "opportunity" a secret from the people around them. This allows for more effective manipulation. Speak with

an accountant, lawyer or certified qualified adviser twice before making an investment. Particularly, be wary of salesmen who put pressure on you and promise limited-time discounts. You shouldn't feel pressured to put money down immediately if the investment is genuine. Please allocate the necessary time to ensure you make a well-informed choice.

- **Raise awareness about the importance of mental wellbeing.** Recognize and confront the emotional impact that being deceived by a fraudulent scheme can have on a person's overall emotional and mental state, as it is crucial for their healing. A lot of people don't know the severe harm that certain scams can cause to a person's overall health. Therefore, it is important to educate yourself and those in your surroundings about the psychological impact of being deceived by a financial scam. When people realize that feeling down after uncovering a scam is a common experience, they are less likely to blame themselves. Raising awareness about mental health also means encouraging open discussions about personal encounters with scams and fostering a safe space for people to talk about their experiences. With this type of insight, we learn the psychological strategies utilized by fraudsters to emotionally manipulate and take advantage of people. By developing a sense of empowerment, we become less susceptible to emotional manipulation and gain the ability to educate others in our communities.

Educating Others

The transition from experiencing fraud to becoming a survivor and advocate is an undeniably captivating and life-altering process. After delving into the various aspects of healing, empowerment and resilience in the preceding sections, it becomes evident that the knowledge acquired from challenging experiences holds significant worth. In my humble opinion, I strongly believe that one of the most influential approaches to applying this knowledge is by enlightening others. By sharing our knowledge and personal encounters, we can generate a ripple effect of consciousness that enables individuals to safeguard themselves and their loved ones from becoming targets of fraudulent activities. Consider this: If an individual had provided you with information regarding a specific fraudulent scheme they were familiar with, the likelihood of you becoming a victim of said scheme would significantly decrease as you would be able to identify the warning signs more promptly. Here are some effective strategies;

- **Share your knowledge with loved ones, relatives, and intimate connections.** In my opinion, no one would want a person to whom they are close to become a target of fraudulent activities, particularly if you have already been deceived yourself. One effective approach to safeguarding your loved ones against possible fraud is telling them about preventive measures. Nevertheless, accomplishing this task is far from simple. Sometimes, getting certain knowledge to stick with individuals can be quite challenging, even if it is beneficial for them. Hence, I suggest you start by selecting the appropriate moment and location to address the topic. When communicating, it is important to ensure that you have the undivided attention of your audience and can express yourself without any disruptions. Start by conveying your worry for their welfare. Make it clear to them that you prioritize their financial wellbeing and ensure that you lead by example. By adhering to recommended guidelines for deterring fraud, you can set a positive example for your loved ones, potentially influencing them to adopt similar practices.

- **Leverage the power of social media, blogs and various online platforms to maximize your reach.** In today's digitally connected society, information regarding fraud prevention has become significantly more accessible to a wider range of individuals. To start off, it is important to determine the social media platforms and online channels that best cater to your target audience. Consider utilizing well-known social media platforms such as Facebook, Twitter, Instagram, LinkedIn or YouTube, alongside blogging platforms like WordPress or Medium. Furthermore, it is important to acknowledge that individuals nowadays possess limited attention spans, largely due to constant overstimulation. Therefore, it is crucial to generate content that is not only informative and engaging, but also tailored to the specific interests, attention spans and needs of your target audience. The types of content that can be included are articles, blog posts, videos, infographics and social media posts. To accommodate various preferences, employ a combination of content formats.
- **Maintain a sense of continuity.** For information to truly become ingrained, it often requires repeated exposure and consistent reinforcement. To put it differently, to ensure the interest of your audience, it is important to adhere to a consistent posting timetable. Implementing this strategy will significantly enhance the visibility of your content in users' feeds and foster a greater sense of trust in your brand.

Chapter 7 Summary

In this section, I delved into my newfound insights after experiencing a fraudulent incident. I highlighted the profound impact of gaining wisdom from mistakes, rather than allowing them to hinder personal growth. Despite occasional instances of fear and embarrassment, I experienced a revitalized feeling of wholeness and strength, and I'm prepared to confront future obstacles with optimism. This section of the book vividly illustrates my unwavering dedication to transforming a distressing encounter into a powerful force for constructive transformation. As someone who doesn't easily back down, my determination to raise awareness about financial scams has only grown stronger after personally falling victim to fraud. I am driven to inform and educate as many individuals as I can by recounting my own experience. I aspire to assist a multitude of individuals in steering clear of the challenges I faced, and if they encounter similar obstacles, to recognize that these experiences do not shape their identity. Moreover, this chapter highlighted the importance of spreading knowledge regarding emotional health, and wrapped up by offering practical tips on safeguarding finances, advocating for prudence, utilizing secure means of communication, seeking diverse perspectives prior to taking action and fostering a culture of mental wellness.

CONCLUSION

Opportunities can be found within every challenging situation.

– Albert Einstein

I wrote this book with the intention of assisting those who have fallen victim to fraud. I aim to convey that there is a future ahead, no matter how bleak things may seem. During my darkest days, as I struggled to find a way out, I searched for guidance in books and resources but found very little available. Fraud is a topic that often remains hushed and brushed under the rug. It's not discussed openly enough, and victims are sometimes unfairly labeled as foolish or unintelligent, compounding the feelings they already grapple with.

We must disseminate more information about the various types of fraud and demystify the subject. It's crucial to shift the focus away from shaming victims and instead provide the necessary support for their recovery.

If the sole outcome of reading this book is that it spares one person from experiencing the heartache I endured, I will be content. I will be overjoyed if it goes beyond that and saves more than one person. It would mean that my words have positively impacted and supported someone during difficult times. I hope those who have been victims of fraud sense that they have a community of individuals who will offer guidance and unwavering support during their most challenging moments.

After enduring several years of hardship, including fraud and personal family loss, I've come to understand that the narrative I once believed, which portrayed me as a worthless person whose life was over, was completely unfounded. I now believe that my life is experiencing a fresh start, with the fraud incident catalyzing a thrilling new adventure. My motivation and ambition have surged, surpassing what I felt in my 30s. It feels as if I'm 19 once more, embarking on a new and exciting journey. The key lesson from my story is that, irrespective of your previous experiences, you can begin shaping a fresh reality starting today.

Fraud can affect anyone, regardless of their intelligence or social standing. It is not selective; it targets everyone. We should not view fraud as the victim's fault but as the perpetrator's fault. It should not be a hidden issue; instead, it should be openly discussed and addressed. Victims of fraud should receive the same warmth and empathy as victims of other crimes.

Sadly, the current environment does not always encourage this. Victims often feel reluctant to confide in friends and family or report to the police, unlike victims of other crimes like burglary, who usually feel more comfortable seeking support. Change is needed, and it's needed urgently.

I am deeply passionate about this cause and will not cease my efforts until the public understands why. Victims of fraud should receive the same treatment as other crime victims, and support should be accessible to them, regardless of where they are in the world.

Having said all that, I take great pride in the woman I have become. Despite enduring traumatic life experiences, I have emerged stronger and with a more enlightened perspective on life. I am committed to ongoing growth and learning from my experiences, ensuring that my family's future is characterized by success rather than fraud.

A fraud victim's strength shines brightest when they rebuild their life from the ruins of deceit.

REFERENCES

Cherry, K. (2022). *What is the halo effect?* https://www.verywellmind.com/what-is-the- halo-effect-2795906

Eeles, M. (2023). *What is an investment syndicate?* https://www.linkedin.com/pulse/what- investment-syndicate-martyn-eeles/

Federal Trade Commission. (2009). *Guides Concerning the Use of Endorsements and Testimonials in Advertising*. https://www.ftc.gov/sites/default/files/attach ments/press-releases/ftc-publishes-final-guides- governing-endorsements-testimonials/091005revisedendorsementguides. pdf

Federal Trade Commission. (2022). *New data shows FTC received 2.8 million fraud reports from consumers in 2021*. https://www.ftc.gov/news-events/news/press-releases/2022/02/new-data-shows-ftc-received-28-million-fraud-reports-consumers-2021-0

Ford. H. (n.d.). *Henry Ford quotes*. https://www.brainyquote.com/quotes/henry_f ord_132651

Heraclitus. (n.d.). *Heraclitus quotes*. https://www.brainyquote.com/quotes/heraclit us_107157

Hill, N. (n.d.). *Napoleon Hill quotes*. https://www.brainyquote.com/quotes/napoleo n_hill_121336

Horace. (n.d.). *Horace quotes*. https://www.brainyquote.com/quotes/horace_ 101258

La Bruyère, J.D. (n.d.). *Jean de La Bruyère quotes*. https://www.brainyquote.com/quotes/jean_de_la_bruyere_380158

Mandela, N. (n.d.). *Nelson Mandela quotes.* https://online.visual- paradigm.com/flipbook- maker/templates/quotes/the-greatest-glory-in- living-lies-not-in-never-falling-but-in-rising- every-time-we-fall-nelson-mandela/

McCrea, S. M. (2010). Intuition, insight, and the right hemisphere: Emergence of higher sociocognitive functions. *Psychology Research and Behavior Management*, 1–1. https://doi.org/10.2147/prbm.s7935

Psychology Today (2019). *Dark triad.* https://www.psychologytoday.com/gb/basic/darktriad#:~:text=The%20term%20%E2%80%9CDark%20Triad%E2%80%9D%20refers,Paulhu s%20and%20Kevin%20M

Murakami, H. (2014). *Haruki Murakami quotes.* https://www.vagabondphotography.ca/2014/0 6/01/when-you-come-out-of-the-storm-you- wont-be-the-same-person-who-walked-in- haruki-murakami/

The Knowledge. (2022). *The expert is always right? Authority Bias.* https://www.theknowledge.io/authority-bias/#:~:text=People%20are%20more%20likel y%20to,questioning%20them%20or%20consid ering%20facts

Weber, R. (n.d.). *Ron Weber quotes.* https://www.azquotes.com/quote/1089162

ABOUT CHERISH EDITIONS

Cherish Editions is a bespoke publishing service for authors of mental health, wellbeing and inspirational books.

As a division of Trigger Publishing, the UK's leading independent mental health and wellbeing publisher, we are experienced in creating and selling positive, responsible, important and inspirational books, which work to de-stigmatize the issues around mental health and improve the mental health and wellbeing of those who read our titles.

Founded by Adam Shaw, a mental health advocate, author and philanthropist, and leading psychologist Lauren Callaghan, Cherish Editions aims to publish books that provide advice, support and inspiration. We nurture our authors so that their stories can unfurl on the page, helping them to share their uplifting and moving stories.

Cherish Editions is unique in that a percentage of the profits from the sale of our books goes directly to leading mental health charity Shawmind, to deliver its vision to provide support for those experiencing mental ill health.

Find out more about Cherish Editions by visiting cherisheditions.com or joining us on:

Twitter @cherisheditions
Facebook @cherisheditions
Instagram @cherisheditions

Cherish
EDITIONS

ABOUT SHAWMIND

A proportion of profits from the sale of all Trigger books go to their sister charity, Shawmind, also founded by Adam Shaw and Lauren Callaghan. The charity aims to ensure that everyone has access to mental health resources whenever they need them.

Find out more about the work Shawmind do by visiting shawmind.org or joining them on:

Twitter @Shawmind_
Facebook @ShawmindUK
Instagram @Shawmind_

Shawmind
Your Local Mental Health & Wellbeing Charity

www.ingramcontent.com/pod-product-compliance
Ingram Content Group UK Ltd.
Pitfield, Milton Keynes, MK11 3LW, UK
UKHW022304260825
462294UK00004B/234

9 781916 920743